This book is to be returned on or before
the last date stamped below

Norwich
The Changing City

Norwich
The Changing City

Neil Storey

breedon **books**
PUBLISHING

First published in Great Britain in 2002 by
The Breedon Books Publishing Company Limited
Breedon House, 3 The Parker Centre,
Derby, DE21 4SZ.

ISBN 1 85983 302 0

Printed and bound by Butler & Tanner, Frome, Somerset, England.

Cover printing by Lawrence-Allen Colour Printers, Weston-super-Mare,
Somerset, England.

CONTENTS

Introduction   6

Timeline   8

St Stephen's to Orford Place   9

Cattle Market to Surrey Street   27

Market Place to the Haymarket   47

Back of the Inns to London Street   65

Redwell Street and Prince of Wales Road to Carrow Bridge   81

Riverside to Palace Plain   93

King Street and Magdalen Street to Anglia Square   105

Elm Hill to St Benedict's   125

Duke Street and Grapes Hill to Bethel Street   139

INTRODUCTION

NORWICH is a living, vital city housed in a heartland of tradition and history. Much has changed, much has been lost in the wake of progress and yet the anomaly is that the city retains its delightful character and all pervading atmosphere of a city of obvious antiquity and proud provincial identity. Much of the city's atmosphere of the past is provided by the most obvious and visible monuments to the city's lineage; namely the Norman cathedral with its magnificent spire and the Norman castle set high on its mount. This theme is further endorsed by over 50 extant mediaeval churches and religious houses dispersed across the city, along with numerous half-timbered and gabled buildings which apparently vie for position alongside 19th and 20th-century buildings. But hold fast, cast your eyes above street level and see that many of the later 'buildings' below are merely modern shop fronts on buildings that, in fact, date back to the 16th and 17th century that received 18th-century fascias, features and furniture.

Throughout the 20th century many of what are now considered the historic features of Norwich faced destruction by council order, demolition in response to demand for civic improvement, obliteration by enemy action in war, or were simply in the way of the construction of the inner link road in the 1960s and early 1970s. This last debacle probably wiped away and damaged more historical buildings and sites than the previous three put together!

In the late 19th century much of Norwich still reflected the grid pattern of streets typical of its mediaeval developers. We must remember however, that at this time the city was not the idyllic 'City of Orchards' as described by Fuller nor was it the city of quaint garrets, courts and lanes as sketched by artists. In the late 19th century 80,000 people were crammed into housing within the old city walls; a contemporary social survey stated 'In the courts and yards, which number 749, are to be found housing conditions as bad and insanitary perhaps as those to be found anywhere…'.

The 19th century saw a number of dramatic changes that impacted on and set the pace for the 20th century. The pressure of numbers within the old city walls saw the better paid workers moving out to the new suburbs like Thorpe Hamlet and the lines of terraced houses spreading beyond the city walls. Whole new streets like Duke Street and Prince of Wales Road were forged through residential areas where not even a trackway existed before and at the turn of the century the installation of the tram system pushed through old buildings and streets, creating a new road system all over the city.

After World War One, Norwich City Council were one of the few official bodies to actually set out to build the 'Land Fit for Heroes' promised to the servicemen of what had become known as the Great War. The city's and indeed the country's first council estate was begun at Mile Cross in 1918 and throughout the 1920s and '30s, numerous public works schemes kept hundreds of Norwich men at work in the Depression. Slums were cleared and new houses and flats erected in their place, bridges were renewed and derelict land and open spaces were landscaped into parks under the keen eye of the Parks Superintendent Captain Sandys Winch. All of these were opened with suitable civic pomp; Edward, Prince of Wales visited the city no less than 11 times during this period to open public works projects including Eaton Park and Carrow Bridge. The crowning glory of the city's public works were the City Hall and Market Place opened by HM King George VI and Queen Elizabeth in 1938, it is one of the finest examples of inter-war years architecture in the country.

During World War Two poor old Norwich took a real battering, particularly in what became known as the 'Baedeker Blitz' of 1942 when Hitler targeted cities of historical interest for his firebombs in an attempt to break morale. Whole streets were damaged and devastated, some essential buildings like churches and pubs were lost forever and a number of prime location city centre shops were bombed out and their sites became static water tanks for the duration.

After the war a great feeling of building the city

anew was embodied in the Norwich City Plan of 1946. Grand boulevards and open spaces were planned to sweep across the Haymarket and Gentleman's Walk. In fact the plans went too far and luckily they were never enacted in full. To get an idea of what was planned for the majority of the city centre just look at Hay Hill – I know what I prefer.

In the late 1950s and '60s as the country got back on its feet people began to look around the city with a new pride in the shops and old buildings which surrounded them. A great 'Civic Experiment' was carried out on the Magdalen Street area; people began to get excited about making the most of the historic features around them and the decaying street on the downward turn was buoyed up again with repainted shop fronts, smartened buildings with night time illumination to pick out their best features. Its success received much acclaim in the press and attracted interest from all across the country.

In the early 1970s an inner link road was ploughed through the city in areas which many believe were far too close to the city centre. A hideous flyover was erected over Magdalen Street and a concrete shopping centre with characterless office buildings erected over Botolph Street to make Anglia Square. The narrow thoroughfare known as Grapes Hill was all but wiped out in the wake of the inner link road's four-lane traffic system crowned on the top with a roundabout which sealed the fate of the dear old Chapel Field Drill Hall. So disparaging were these events they could be seen as kicking the impetus out of the city's historic regeneration for the next 20 years as yet more hideous offices and factories were permitted to be erected over old residential areas.

Now, a saying much bandied around in these parts is, 'What goes around, comes around' and when I was on my travels around the city researching this book, I must say I was very pleasantly surprised to find that many of the post-war factories and unsightly business buildings of our city are being torn down, and attractive buildings built in the style of those demolished and very much in keeping with their few surviving neighbours, are going up in their place. New life is being breathed into the old residential areas like Oak Street and King Street and much interest is being shown in the redevelopment of the Riverside area with its smart bars, restaurants and entertainment centres.

Norwich is regenerating, there is new hope in the 21st century; new housing is being erected in sympathetic styles, the newest of the new public buildings, The Forum, is truly remarkable and a structure the city should be proud of; the city centre and Castle Mall seem to compliment each other and with care the redevelopment of the old Caley's factory on Chapel Field, the city will be further enhanced. The delight of the city to me, however, is it is not only being historically considerate in its forward plans but just by taking a stroll in the early morning along the likes of Upper St Giles, St Benedict's or Magdalen Street the smells and sounds and shop fronts of traditional small businesses in the city are all around you. On still sunny mornings birdsong can surround you and the eight o'clock morning chimes of the great City Hall clock can still be clearly heard on the streets of Norwich and thus, the Norwich of Jonathan Mardle's column in the *Eastern Daily Press* and the nostalgic images of the city captured by the photographer George Swain is not that far away today.

Neil Storey
2002

ACKNOWLEDGEMENTS

I would like to extend my personal thanks to the following without whose generous contribution of advice, knowledge or images this book would not have been so enriched: Dr Vic Morgan, Dr Dave Peacock, Les Downham, George Plunkett, Ian Clark, Andy Archer, Maggie Secker and the listeners of BBC Radio Norfolk.

A very special thanks must be given to the staff of the Eastern Counties Newspaper Library and the Norwich Local Studies Library without whose help this book really would not have been possible. Thanks to all those too numerous to mention here who have contributed to my research over the years, your help, input and support is truly invaluable.

Of course thanks, as ever, must go to Terry Burchell for the usual photographic wonders and last but by no means least to my dear family for their love and their endurance of this temperamental author and all his foibles.

TIMELINE

1900   The Norwich Tramway system was opened on 30 July.

1903   Grand Opera House (later the Hippodrome) opened.

1905   Statue in honour of the great 17th-century scholar Sir Thomas Browne unveiled on Hay Hill.

1908   Norwich City FC move to their first purpose-built ground, The Nest, on Rosary Road.

1909   Visit of Edward VII, 11,000 children covered Mousehold to sing to him.

1911   King George V made his first official visit as monarch to the city on 22 June.

1912   Bentfield C. Hucks was first man to fly over Norwich. Worst floods of the century hit city.

1914   Outbreak of World War One. Hundreds of men and women from the city join the colours or volunteer for war work.

1918   Armistice, the end of hostilities and a victory for the allies. Mile Cross, first council estate in England begun.

1919   Interment of Norfolk's greatest heroine, Nurse Cavell at Life's Green near the cathedral.

1923   Miss Dorothy Jewson returned first female MP for the city.

1924   Miss Ethel Mary Colman Norwich City's first lady lord mayor appointed.

1926   Norwich city brought almost to a standstill by General Strike.

1927   City War Memorial, designed by Sir Edwin Lutyens RA opened on 8 October.

1929   Walter Rye, great Norwich and Norfolk antiquarian and last mayor of Norwich dies.

1930   Final closure of Pull's Ferry.

1933   Norwich Municipal Airport opened by HRH Prince of Wales on 21 June.

1934   Theatre Royal destroyed by fire (rebuilt and reopened on 30 September 1935).

1935   Closure of Norwich tramways on 10 December.

1938   Opening of New City Hall and Market Place by HM King George VI and Queen Elizabeth on 29 October.

1939   War declared with Germany. Slit trenches and air raid shelters dug in public parks, public buildings boarded up and sandbagged.

Aerial view of St Peter Mancroft and the old area of lanes between Theatre Street and Bethel Street c.1937.

1940   First air raid on Norwich on 9 July.

1942   The 'Baedeker Blitz', the worst the city saw throughout the war.

1945   Peace celebrations in the Market Place with end of the war in Germany in May and in the Far East in August.

1949   Great Norwich character William Cullum 'Billy Bluelight' dies aged 90.

1959   Anglia TV goes on air.

1963   University of East Anglia opens.

1964   Last speedway meeting at The Firs.

1970   Last-ever brew prepared at Steward & Patteson's Pockthorpe Brewery.

1977   HM Queen Elizabeth II visits during her silver jubilee year on 11 July.

1987   Norwich City Sports Village opens.

1988   New law courts opened.

1993   The Mall Shopping Centre opened.

1994   Norwich celebrates 800 years since Richard I granted its self-government Charter.

1996   Norwich Cathedral celebrates its 900th anniversary.

2000   The charred remains of the old library cleared and foundations of Millennium Library laid and finally opened to the public in 2001.

Aerial view of Norwich Castle, stronghold of the city for over 900 years c.1937.

St Stephen's to Orford Place

St Stephen's Gate, drawn here by John Ninham in 1792, was one of 12 city gates erected as part of the 'New Defences' introduced between 1297 and 1344. A large proportion of the cost of these works was met by wealthy city merchant Richard Spynk. St Stephen's was the main entrance gate for those travelling to and from Norwich to London. Richly decorated, it was through here that Elizabeth I entered Norwich on her Royal Progress in 1578. In later years it was inhabited by a hermit who paid 8s 6d per annum. In 1793 the gate was demolished as part of the city 'improvements'.

The Boileau Memorial and Fountain at the junction of Ipswich and Newmarket Roads *c.*1950. Within the four-arch, four-pedimented cover is a drinking fountain surmounted by a statue of a woman and child, entitled 'Charity'. Erected by Sir Raymond Boileau as a memorial to his wife Catherine in 1874; the female figure designed by Sir Joseph Boehm is said to be based on Lady Catherine herself. The brick canopy was removed in the 1956 leaving the beautiful statue looking rather lost in the middle of an increasingly busy road. Under the final road-widening scheme in 1967 the fountain was removed and the statue placed in the grounds of the Norfolk and Norwich Hospital where it remains today.

The Norfolk and Norwich Hospital 1959. Founded in 1771 the present buildings were erected on part of the original site and were formally opened in 1882. The foundation stone of these new buildings had been laid in June 1879 by HM King Edward VII when he was Prince of Wales. Constructed to designs by Boardman and Wyatt, architects of Norwich and London, the fully-fitted building cost a total of £57,116. Just over 100 years later, the new, multi-million pound Norfolk and Norwich Hospital has recently opened at Colney.

The Great Eastern Railway's Victoria Station situated between St Stephen's Road, Queens Road and Grove Road. Built on the site of the Ranelagh Gardens by the Eastern Union Railway Company it was formally opened in 1849 and was later taken over by the Great Eastern Railway. From here thousands left in the summer months for the coast, their queues spilling round onto Queens Road; in the early years of World War One soldiers departed here for their war stations. Through the demands of war the station became dedicated to goods traffic and closed to passengers in 1916.

Victoria Station goods yard c.1960. Passenger services never returned to Victoria Station. The station buildings were demolished and the platforms removed to make way for concreted areas for goods vehicles. Finally closed in the mid-1960s, today the old station site is occupied by a tall office block and the goods yard by a supermarket.

St Stephen's Street and Queen's Road *c*.1955. On the right may be seen the Great Eastern public house, the last pub in Norwich to have a 5am licence for the benefit of early morning workers. The favourite tipple sold at this hour was known as 'early purl' a hot spiced beer laced with wormwood. This whole scene was to be changed beyond recognition in the early 1960s.

As early as 1931 plans for a road-widening scheme had been proposed for St Stephen's Street and this was prevented only by the intervention of the Society for the Protection of Ancient Buildings. However, the damage inflicted in the bombing of 1942, coupled with renewed pressure for road-widening and redevelopment from the mid-1950s, sealed the fate of St Stephen's. Pictured about 1965, here on the site of the Great Eastern pub stands a multi-storey car park and a Keymarket's food store.

Laying tram tracks on St Stephen's Street 1899. Once the planned city centre routes of the tramway were cleared, the tracks were laid. Along St Stephen's a double track was laid to enable the free flow of passing trams along this busy route. Once completed the tram system comprised a total of 19 miles, 2 furlongs and 100 yards of rails.

Still retaining its Victorian character of pull-down shutter and multi-panelled shop windows this is St Stephen's Street c.1938. Among the shops on the left are James Cook's chemist, Kingston's butchers, Nicholl's provision dealers, and Lionel Thirkettle's pork butchers, while on the right is the Crown and Angel pub, kept by Frank Hall, and Thirkettle's butchers (yes, he did have a shop on each side of the road), Brighter Homes Stores wallpaper merchants.

The Boar's Head Tavern on the corner of Surrey Street and St Stephen's *c.*1938. An ale house stood here for over 500 years. It was known in the 17th and 18th centuries as the Greyhound but as reading in those days was mostly a preserve of the upper classes the pub was eventually renamed after the common name it was given. Derived from the heraldic device of the Norgate family, who displayed their arms above the door of pub they owned in the 1790s, it became known as the Boar's Head.

St Stephen's Street 1942. On the right is the burnt out shell of the pub beloved as the snug of farmers visiting the cattle market – the Boar's Head. Almost every building on St Stephen's was damaged, some extensively during the nights of 27-28 and 29-30 April 1942. Hitler had unleashed what became known as the Baedeker Blitz, named after the famous guide books, these attacks consisting predominantly of incendiary bomb drops focussed on the historical cities of England in an attempt to break morale.

St Stephen's Street, July 1963. Post-war rebuilding on bomb sites through the 1950s led to the road- widening scheme and redevelopment of the entire street in the 1960s. On this side of the road a handful of the pre-war shops remain while modern shops take the place of their neighbours. On the opposite side of the road the widening scheme saw complete redevelopment from the conversion of the rebuilt Boar's Head to offices, to the demolition of the Great Eastern pub.

St Stephen's Street today. Still one of the busiest streets in Norwich for both trade and traffic. A far cry from when Queen Elizabeth I entered the city with full processional honours here in 1578, and of course a world away from the street just wide enough for two trams to pass and affectionately remembered by city dwellers from before World War Two.

St Stephen's Plain c.1890. On the left is the old Bunting's store. Remembered as a veritable rabbit warren, this department store had spread through the neighbouring shops as Arthur Bunting purchased them to expand his drapery business begun in 1866. Also seen here is the Peacock pub which stood next to the famous Deacon's fish restaurant, built in the 1930s. Sadly the pub with the grand frontage was eventually demolished to make way for modern retail premises.

Bunting's new department store c.1912. Eventually Mr Bunting had the old buildings, into which he had gradually expanded, torn down and a brand new, purpose-built department store erected. Designed by Augustus Scott it was one of the first buildings in the city to be built of reinforced concrete. Burnt to a shell in the Baedeker Blitz of April 1942 Buntings moved their business to London Street. The old building was refitted to become a NAAFI complete with theatre, ballroom, tavern, dining hall and writing room. With its Scott frontage intact today it is still a popular department store occupied by Marks and Spencer.

F.W. Woolworth's first store on Rampant Horse Street *c.*1922. Known as the '3d and 6d store', they moved to the opposite side of the road where their store remained until the 1990s when Marks and Spencer expanded their food hall and clothing department over the site. The building seen here was sold to the expanding Curls Brothers drapers and furnishers. With this purchase Curls now owned the entire left-hand side of Red Lion Street between Rampant Horse Back Street and Rampant Horse Street. This building was destroyed during the Baedeker Blitz, 28-29 and 29-30 April 1942.

A final look back at St Stephen's Plain viewed from Rampant Horse Street *c.*1955. Originally just a raised wooden platform and hand rail, after a few near misses the St Stephen's 'point' is seen here with its distinctive stripy skirt and PC Gordon Hare on duty. A police presence was maintained here every day between 8am and 6pm until 1964 when the 'point' was replaced by traffic lights.

Rampant Horse Street decked out with banners and bunting on King George V's silver jubilee day Monday 6 May 1935. Some of the events in the 100-page souvenir booklet which outlined the week's festivities included a grand street procession, distribution of medals and cartons of chocolates to schoolchildren, a united service in the cathedral and selections of music performed by bands in the Norwich parks.

The devastation of Rampant Horse Street viewed from the churchyard of St Stephen's Church on the morning of 30 April 1942. Curls store, Buntings and Boots the Chemist have been reduced to rubble and burnt out shells along with their neighbours in this area which over two nights of hell received the worst damage of any area in the city centre throughout the war.

Out of the cleared bomb site, which had served as a static water tank and car park in the meantime, on the corner of Rampant Horse Street and Red Lion Street the scaffolding begins to rise as Curls store is built anew in 1955. Curls became a familiar feature of the city's shopping scene once again. Still a department store of the highest standard today, it was taken over by Debenham's in the early 1970s.

Red Lion Street looking towards St Stephen's Plain *c.*1890. All of the buildings on the left were regarded by the late Victorians as unsightly slums and beyond repair or modernisation, so the decision was taken to demolish all of them in the 1890s. Among the buildings lost was the Red Lion pub from which the road took its name. This old hostelry was a popular spot for city revelries after the Restoration when 'plays and drolls' were performed there.

Gone are the old shambles and in their place are the newly-completed Anchor Buildings, built to the visionary designs of city architect George Skipper *c.*1900. A magnificent improvement to Red Lion Street, the buildings are pictured when they were newly erected. The road has become an open space and the tram terminus would soon be constructed in the foreground.

Orford Place tram terminus shortly after its opening on 30 July 1900. The opening was a grand occasion and crowds rejoiced here until gone midnight while women 'forgot all modesty' as they leaned out of bedroom windows to watch the trams pass. Trams were regarded by the Edwardians as great progress, providing the city with decent roads instead of dirty and dusty trackways, as well as being a cheap and efficient method of transport.

The junction of Rampant Horse Back Street with Red Lion Street to the right c.1885. Once this area made a little triangulated island near Orford Place; another left turn a few hundred yards up Red Lion Street was Little Orford Street; the point of the triangle was made by the Goose and Grid Iron pub where the two roads converged at the rear. The road 'improvements' for the trams and the expansion of Curls store brought about the total destruction and disappearance of Rampant Horse Back Street and just about every dwelling and shop on this photograph.

The Norfolk & Norwich Savings Bank, built in 1844 on the corner of the Haymarket, and just beyond the point of the Goose and Grid Iron pub, photographed in 1898. To the right may be seen the one-time home of the eminent Norwich doctor and philosopher, Sir Thomas Browne (1605-82). Both these buildings were unceremoniously torn down in 1899 when the tram routes were implemented.

Little Orford Street pictured shortly after the demolition of the Goose and Grid Iron for the tram route being cut in to the left c.1899. Piled up in front of Curls store are the blocks for the new road surface. Next door to that is John Nickalls, glass, china and earthenware dealer. The Gothic chapel-like building next door is the original 1888 Church of England Young Men's Christian Association premises which also acted as the Norwich headquarters of the St John Ambulance Association. On the right is George Smith's seed merchants.

Little Orford Street, 1954. On the left the hoardings are up for the rebuilding and expansion of Curls store which involved the demolition of the old Church of England Young Men's Christian Association building. In the background is Burton's outfitters, who moved further down the Walk, and the Haymarket cinema, both of which were demolished in 1959 to make way for a series of modern shops. This little road is now reduced to a rather narrow footway and it is hard to imagine traffic – especially a bus – ever flowing through here.

AN ACTION-PACKED WEEK AT THE

ORFORD CELLAR

WEDNESDAY OCTOBER 12th

The Cream with

ERIC CLAPTON

GINGER BAKER

JACK BRUCE

SUNDAY-Your only chance to hear the man
who put "BARE FOOTIN" in the Charts

Robert Parker

With Stevie Winwood's Discoveries

WYNDER K. FROGG

Don't Miss This Great Night Out !
It's A Ram Jam Rave !

Another Great **DISCOTHEQUE SESSION**
ON FRIDAY
SATURDAY
Features The Drifters Backing
Group

THE MOTIVATION

All Session from 8 p.m.
Come Early to Avoid Disappointment

In more recent times this area is best remembered for the music venue under the street known as The Orford Cellar. In the 1960s the *Evening News* was eagerly scanned for the bands appearing at this venue. It is hard to imagine today but many of the big names of the day played here, including Jimi Hendrix, David Bowie and, as seen on this handbill from 1966, The Cream with Eric Clapton, Ginger Baker and Jack Bruce.

The Bell Hotel and Orford Hill *c.*1895. One of the city's last surviving coaching inns, an alehouse has been on this site since the 15th century. Once known as the Blue Bell, many unusual clubs met here in the 18th century; among them were the Hellfire Club, whose members arranged the stoning and jeering of the Wesley brothers when they came to preach on Orford Hill, and the Revolution Club, founded in 1793. This club caused so much concern that it was investigated by a government inspector who declared that its membership were not of danger to the security of the country but were businessmen 'of the lowest description'.

Trams on Orford Hill with Back of the Inns in the background *c.*1931. The cut for traffic to pass directly on to Castle Meadow was made possible by the demolition of Clarke's ironmonger's shop, which stood beside the Bell Hotel, in 1899. When this photograph was taken the death knell for trams in the city was already sounding. In 1933 it emerged that the Eastern Counties Omnibus Company had bought a controlling interest in the tramway company and had begun the necessary legal procedures to bring about the abandonment of trams in Norwich.

The Bell Hotel and Orford Hill, 1959. Although the trams are gone, the gap was retained to allow the free flow of traffic through the city. Today traffic has increased to such an extent that this area is now for one-way traffic only.

The Bell Hotel, Orford Hill, and Timberhill, 1971. Gone today is the little car park on Orford Hill. Cobbled and provided with benches, this area is now pedestrianised with limited vehicle access. On the right of the photograph is the long-established Darlow's gunmakers with the unique figurehead on the city skyline – a life-size metal stag.

W. & G. Boston's pawnbrokers, Orford Hill, 1964. From the 1850s and for over 100 years, the family name of Boston was synonymous with Orford Hill. George Boston & Sons were complete house, hotel, theatre and cinema furnishers, cabinet makers and baby-carriage specialists. Thomas Boston were clothiers, while William and Geoffrey Boston's pawnbrokers, established in 1856, was the longest-lived business, surviving into the 1980s.

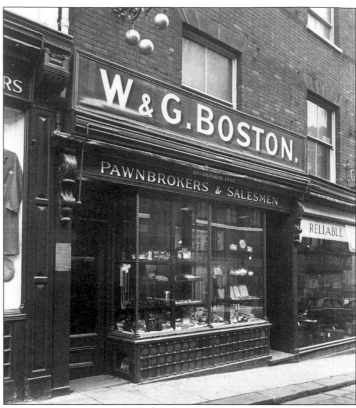

Inside W. & G. Boston's pawnbrokers in 1964. In front of a backdrop of the larger pledges such as blankets and fine cloths, Alan Gayford casts an expert eye over a fine salver – but is it silver or plate? This shop and the cornucopia of things brought in could tell a thousand stories; from people so poor they kept a 'rolling pledge' to keep food on the table from one week to the next, to the men who would pawn their war medals, redeeming them once a year for Armistice Day. Although the shop no longer exists the interior has been moved and preserved exactly as seen here in the Bridewell Museum, dedicated to Norfolk life.

CATTLE MARKET TO SURREY STREET

Taken on Saturday 25 June 1960 this photograph shows the last cattle market held near the castle. In the pens by Ireland's sale rooms, who had traded on the cattle market for 130 years, may be seen the last of the fat cattle to be sold. The sales were moved to the purpose-built livestock market at Harford Bridges on the southern outskirts of the city.

William Clarke's ironmonger's shop which faced Castle Meadow *c.*1895. To the left of the shop is the Bell Hotel, while to the right are buildings adjoining Castle Meadow and Back of the Inns. In 1899 this shop and a few of the buildings to the right were demolished to allow a clear passage for the new tram system from Orford Place through to Castle Meadow.

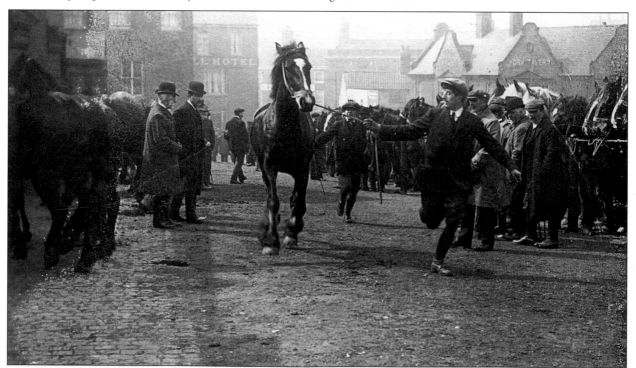

Trotting horses up Bell Avenue for Spelman's horse sale *c.*1908. Horse sales were a familiar feature of the Norwich market calendar for generations. Messrs Spelmans conducted their first sale in the Castle Ditches in 1825. The sales moved to Bell Avenue 27 years later where they remained until 1933 when they were relocated to Walton's Yard on Golden Ball Street.

Norwich Castle *c*.1903. Originally a wooden structure built shortly after the Norman Conquest, the stone castle was erected between 1120-30. In 1220 it became the county gaol, a role it carried out continuously for almost 700 years. The castle was refaced in Bath stone in the 1830s, keeping the form and detail of the Normans faithfully but little attempt was made to retain its 'old lively texture'. The old gaol closed in 1887 and the prisoners removed to the new gaol on Mousehold. In 1894 the castle was reopened as a museum and art gallery a role it fills today after a multi-million pound refit.

In the 'grand old days' of Norwich cattle market, in the 1930s, here we see the full sheep pens with a sale in progress. In 1935 a total of 212,000 head of stock were sold here with sales of over £1,250,000 per annum.

Auction shed, cattle and pens at the rear of the Agricultural Hall *c.*1935. This was just one small part of the old cattle market site which spread over almost nine acres; in its day it was one of the largest in the country. Today this busy yet traditional agricultural scene, so indicative of the ways things were done in bygone days, has been lost forever. The pens and shed have been removed. Immediately behind the Agricultural Hall, now part of the Anglia Television complex, the area is grassed, while a busy multi-lane road system files traffic into the Castle Mall or on toward Shirehall Plain.

What am I bid? In the sale pens at Norwich cattle market, November 1958. The smell on a wet day was an unforgettable and potent blend of the steaming stock being sold, damp raincoats and tobacco.

A once-familiar scene outside one of the auction sheds on Norwich cattle market *c.*1948. Waiting on the road are the cattle trucks which took the noisy livestock to and from market. Up until just a few years before the cattle market closed, cattle were still to be seen being driven along the city streets; some had been walked from farms on the outskirts of the city while others were walked to and from the railways stations. The men doing the job were known as drovers and they would recruit boys armed with sticks along the way to go 'bullock whopping' – keeping the cattle from straying off the roads.

The Shirehall viewed over empty cattle pens *c.*1910. Connected to the castle by a winding staircase and passageways originally erected in 1822, it was then known as the Shire House. Here, the assizes and quarter sessions for the county, as well as the County Court were held. The hall was enlarged in 1887 to provide waiting rooms for witnesses with 21 cells for males and four waiting cells for females. The photograph shows the newly completed extension beside the Shirehall built for County Council departments between 1908-9. Today the Shirehall is the Regimental Museum of the Royal Norfolk Regiment.

Suits you sir! Fitting 'buskins' – leather leggings popularly used by agricultural workers – on Norwich cattle market, October 1951.

Once Spelman's horse sale had moved to Golden Ball Street in 1933 their vacant auction sheds were demolished to make way for this coach and car park photographed shortly after it opened in 1934.

Bell Avenue, February 1985. A popular stopping point for tourist coaches, here were based a number of travel centres and shops, most affectionately remembered of these being the pet shop. This shop provided thousands of city kids with their first pet rabbit or guinea pig. Stocked with a veritable menagerie of pets from fish to birds, many folks remember the cheeky mynah bird put outside in his cage on summer days. Opposite these shops was the centre of the old cattle market. With its pens removed, this cobbled site lent itself easily to its new role as an open-air city centre car park. All this has been lost or changed in the wake of the Castle Mall development.

Construction of the Castle Mall in full swing, May 1991. The view is taken from Farmer's Avenue with the site of Bell Avenue on the left, all that remained of the structures here were the castle gatehouses. Beneath them may be seen the earlier flint gatehouse ruins uncovered by the development.

The Castle Meadow, entrance to the Castle Mall shopping centre. Completed in September 1993, the mall development occupies nearly seven acres of the old Cattle Market site and is a multi-level complex which cost £75 million within a total development cost of £145 million. Although a huge investment, it is proving to be a valuable addition to Norwich's commercial life.

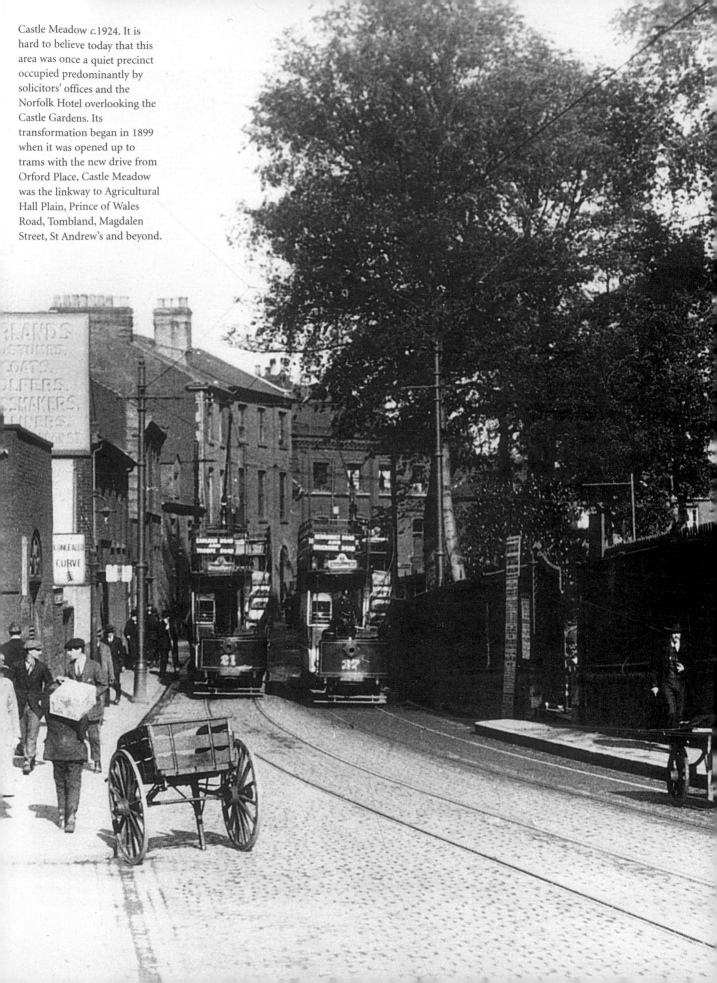

Castle Meadow *c*.1924. It is hard to believe today that this area was once a quiet precinct occupied predominantly by solicitors' offices and the Norfolk Hotel overlooking the Castle Gardens. Its transformation began in 1899 when it was opened up to trams with the new drive from Orford Place, Castle Meadow was the linkway to Agricultural Hall Plain, Prince of Wales Road, Tombland, Magdalen Street, St Andrew's and beyond.

Widening Castle Meadow, 1927. As traffic grew on Tombland the road had to be widened, there was barely enough room in places for trams to pass, pedestrians on the castle side feared for their lives as trams rattled past, let alone adding motor cars to the equation. A road-widening scheme was enacted between the years 1926 and 1927 to alleviate the problem.

Resurfacing Castle Meadow c.1950. After the tram tracks were removed in the 1930s their furrows were filled in with chippings and tar leaving a very uneven surface on one of the busiest roads in the city. As part of the city improvements after World War Two the surface was completely removed and a new surface laid. Limiting the traffic through this busy street presented many problems so work had to be carried out apace with between 36 to 40 tons of hot asphalt being laid each week.

Rose Lane c.1880. An area of the city once renowned for its gardens the quiet lane grew into a bustling road connecting the cattle market to the new railway station in 1844. Once extending to Foundry Bridge this end of Rose Lane was swallowed up with the construction of the lower portion of Prince of Wales Road in 1862. Today part of the inner link road Rose Lane is one-way and sees the flow of thousands of cars along its three traffic lanes every day.

The interior of Clowes & Nash's poultry mart on Market Avenue c.1935. In May 1933 the new market was opened with room to display 3,000 head of poultry and it was estimated 152,874 birds were exhibited for sale in the first year of business. It was also at this time that Clowes & Nash worked together with Warren & Ling, auctioneers to organise the first turkey sale on Norwich cattle market.

Market Avenue leading up to Golden Ball Street, the Golden Ball pub may be seen with its distinctive spherical sign on the corner, *c*.1964. The Buff Coat, whose name alludes to the type of jackets worn by Cromwellian soldiers, was a great haunt of the drovers and carters of the Norwich markets. Once the cattle market moved away, trade never recovered and the Buff Coat closed in 1964. All of these buildings were demolished to make way for Rouen Road and the ECN Building in the late 1960s.

A wonderful view, dating from about 1875, from the junction of Golden Ball Street and Market Avenue, looking across the Cattle Market. The market had been railed and paved in 1861 and many of the young trees seen here had been provided by the 'Mustard King', J.J. Colman, from his own estate to provide shade for the beasts on sale. Most of the trees have been swept away, if not by time then by the building of the Castle Mall, which occupies most of this view today.

Golden Ball Street 1930. All the shops on the right have now disappeared, most of them in a road-widening scheme in 1938. Just up the road from Ernest Howard's barber's shop – denoted by the traditional red and white pole – is the original Woolpack Inn (rebuilt further back in 1938), opposite that once stood the Eagle and Child and up the road the 200-year-old Plough Inn. In the 1860s the street was renowned for its stables and infamous for its pubs – each one with a large pewter chamber pot in the public rooms.

Upper Ber Street c.1935. Up to the turn of the century this road was nicknamed 'Blood and Guts Street' from the stench of offal and running blood from the slaughterhouses by day and the fights by night. Once a colourful area it was home to many of the immigrant population, especially gypsies and Italians. Much of the street seen here, including the church of St Michael-at-Thorn, was destroyed in the 1942 firebomb blitz.

Ber Street looking towards the city 1936. Conditions were not good here at the time. People lived in congested yards where dozens of cottages huddled around a communal water tap. Many of the old slums were destroyed in the 1942 firebomb blitz, those which remained finally met their nemesis in the 1960s when council apartment buildings and flats were put up in their place.

The bottom of Golden Ball Street used to present the traveller with this fork in the road. Centre of the fork, and centre of this photograph taken about 1937, is Thomas Hastings, fruit and potato merchant at No.1 Ber Street. Beside him is Patrick's stores, the 'head to foot outfitters' who spread along 3, 5, 7 and 11 Ber Street. To the right is All Saints' Street, leading to All Saints' Green. Another of the city's shortest streets, in 1937 it consisted of Miss Beatrice Pye's confectioners, Frederick Burrow's watch repairers and Arthur Minns' bakers.

The morning after the air raid of 27 June 1942 when a large swathe of the city suffered a combined incendiary and high explosive bombing raid. To the left may be seen Brooks Flats, Patricks' stores and Hastings fruiterers blown up or severely damaged by a 250kg bomb and incendiary attack which also burnt out St Michael-at-Thorn Church and many surrounding properties.

Known colloquially across the city as Bond's Corner this photograph, taken in February 1965, shows the new Bond's Store built on the bombed-out site of Hastings fruiterers and All Saints' Street. At this time the new tarmac surface contrasted with the old cobbles to denote the old fork in the road.

Westlegate *c.*1890. A charming study of a city street before motor car or tram dominated the roads. Westlegate derives its name from the 'wastels' (white loaves of the finest flour) which were made here until the early 19th century. The fine old gabled, thatched building at the top of the road was the Light Dragoon public house. This pub was always known locally as the Barking Dickey; the derivation of the name, so local folklore tells, was due to the badly painted sign that hung above its door. The Dragoons' steed with its open mouth looked far more like a donkey braying or 'barking' and its body far more like a dog than a warhorse, so the name stuck.

Westlegate, 1964. The structure of the Barking Dickey still stands proud, having served as a restaurant and even a bank, but much of the old Westlegate has gone. The first changes came about as early as 1925 when a road-widening scheme was implemented. Deacon's famous restaurant was extended with butchery and tinned food departments up the road, while smartly-fronted city offices were also built. After the war further developments took place with the demolition of further old and bomb-damaged buildings for this tower of offices and showrooms, built in the 'fashionable' designs of the time and completed in 1964. After serving for a few years as offices the lower showroom was bought and refronted to become Norwich's first McDonalds burger eatery in the 1980s.

All Saints Green c.1915. Until the 18th century the majority of this area was occupied by the old swine market; All Saints Green was simply a small area just in front of the church which rolled up to abut the swine market. The open area of 'the Green' was bounded by Georgian houses with large gardens, some of which were ornamental with fountains and conservatories. Most of these are now removed to make way for offices and those Georgian houses that remain simply act as a screen for the Norwich Union offices. The buildings seen here on the eastern side of the road including the Thatched Theatre Ballroom and Bond's Tudor Stores were all burnt out or blown up during the firebomb blitz on Norwich on 27 June 1942.

Exterior of the Thatched Theatre ballroom, *c*.1910.

Interior of the Thatched Theatre ballroom, All Saint's Green *c*.1910. This elegant ballroom along with its fine restaurant were converted to become the auditorium of the Thatched Theatre in November 1915. The Thatched Theatre was well known for showing the best and classiest films accompanied by string orchestra for the discerning city clientele. Never wired for the talkies, the cinema closed in 1930 and perished with the rest of the buildings in this area during the firebomb blitz of 1941. Today Bond's department store covers the area.

The Carlton Cinema, All Saints' Green *c*.1935. The Carlton, opened in 1932, was the first Norwich cinema to show talking pictures. In 1939 it was bought into the Odeon circuit and its name changed to the Gaumont when the old Gaumont on the Haymarket closed in 1959. Affectionately remembered by many city cinemagoers, events and promotions here included appearances by our local 'Rocket Man' and even Roy Rogers. It closed as a cinema in 1973 to become a bingo club, a purpose it still serves today.

Surrey Street *c*.1905. During the 19th century the houses here were famed for their glasshouses, grape vines, fig trees and magnolias. All of the houses on the right have now disappeared in the wake of 1950s and '60s offices. The destruction had begun as far back as 1903 when Norwich Union replaced the last grand 'city house', Surrey Court, with its head offices. Now every square inch of the grounds have been ploughed back for office accommodation.

Norwich bus station, Surrey Street 1957. Built on the site of Bignold Court in the late 1930s when the bus company moved here from their offices and depot at 79 Thorpe Road. Before World War Two the Norwich Omnibus Company operated over 36 route miles around the city with 88 vehicles and 350 employees.

Your destination please… Norwich bus station booking hall, Surrey Street, 1957. Here coach trips all over the country could be booked giving city folks a chance to travel further than many could have imagined a generation before. In the summer months during the 1950s and early 1960s the stalls would be full of queues of expectant holidaymakers; the ladies in printed floral A-line dresses and cardigans with the gents in sports jackets, blazers, and Fair Isle pullovers while the children, in shorts and pumps or sandals, tried to lick the drips from their rapidly melting ice creams. Happy days!

MARKET PLACE TO THE HAYMARKET

The Guildhall and vegetable market from a lithograph by David Hodgson, 1820. Seen before the Victorian restorations the magnificent east end had not yet acquired its clock turret or buttresses. To the left on the 17th-century flat roof may be seen an Italianate loggia complete with city gentry observing the market. All of the buildings to the left of the Guildhall have been demolished over the years with the final cull coming in the 1930s when it was cleared for the new City Hall and market. Although most of the shop fronts to the right have changed dramatically the façades above have survived remarkably unchanged to the present day.

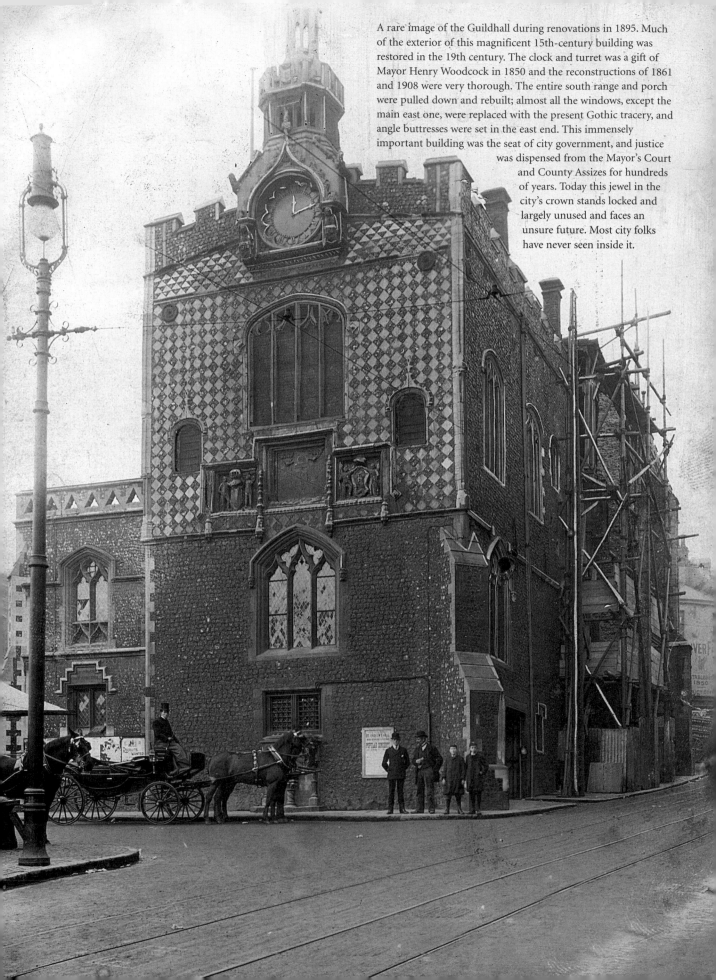

A rare image of the Guildhall during renovations in 1895. Much of the exterior of this magnificent 15th-century building was restored in the 19th century. The clock and turret was a gift of Mayor Henry Woodcock in 1850 and the reconstructions of 1861 and 1908 were very thorough. The entire south range and porch were pulled down and rebuilt; almost all the windows, except the main east one, were replaced with the present Gothic tracery, and angle buttresses were set in the east end. This immensely important building was the seat of city government, and justice was dispensed from the Mayor's Court and County Assizes for hundreds of years. Today this jewel in the city's crown stands locked and largely unused and faces an unsure future. Most city folks have never seen inside it.

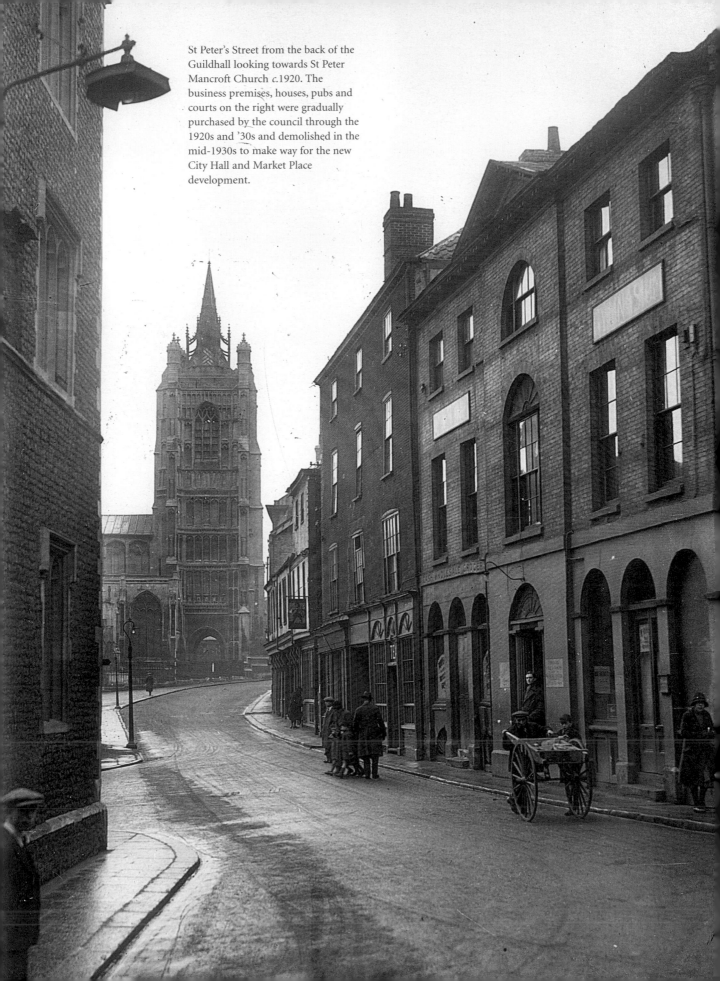

St Peter's Street from the back of the
Guildhall looking towards St Peter
Mancroft Church *c.*1920. The
business premises, houses, pubs and
courts on the right were gradually
purchased by the council through the
1920s and '30s and demolished in the
mid-1930s to make way for the new
City Hall and Market Place
development.

Looking along St Peter's Street towards the Guildhall with the fishmarket on the right *c*.1895. As well evinced by this wonderful old image, many carriers parked their carts here and could be found mardling between themselves while waiting for their return journeys to the outlying towns and villages. It was also the carriers who filled the Georgian pubs such as the Beehive, Wounded Hart (renamed the Kitchener's Arms) and White Hart which stood here. All of this was demolished in the mid-1930s in the wake of the new City Hall and Market Place development.

Guildhall Hill *c*.1899. On the right are the offices of the *Norfolk Chronicle*, once one of the city's oldest surviving newspapers. A little further up the imposing building on the corner of Dove Lane was the new Chamberlin's store built on the site of their premises destroyed in the August Bank Holiday fire disaster of 1898.

Norwich Market Place, *c.*1899, shortly before the coming of the tram system. In front of the row of 'higgledy-piggledy' stalls are some of the carriers' carts which transported people and goods to and from the market. Using village pubs as staging posts, their services were frequently advertised in directories and newspapers, running from rural areas to the city centre and vice-versa. To the left of this photograph may be seen the statue of the Duke of Wellington, erected here in 1854 and removed to Cathedral Close in 1937.

The Market Place and Gentleman's Walk *c.*1925. In this evocative image may be seen passing trams, queues of cabs, bustling streets and a choppy sea of canopies which truly typify the Market Place in the first three decades of the 20th century. In those days the market was cleared away at the end of every trading day, leaving a wide open space ideal for city festivities.

Looking across the Market Place towards St Peter Mancroft from Jarrold's Corner *c.*1922. The grand- looking buildings in the centre were originally pubs but were gradually purchased by the city council for their offices from about 1910. From this view they look lovely but inside a number of rooms were unusable due to weak floors and suffered from severe rat infestation.

Guildhall Hill *c.*1938. Gone are the tram tracks, cobbles and vegetable market to be replaced with a sweeping, open-paved area. On the Hill itself, Chamberlin's department store still dominates the scene, also here at the time were Spall's fancy goods store, Dean & Palmer tailors, Willerby's tailors and the well-remembered Prince's Café.

Blasting off the top of the façade of the old Municipal Buildings in the Market Place *c.*1935. When blasting out the lower levels a great brown mass was seen to swarm across the road; not dust, but rats seeking new homes! Not all was simply destroyed in the demolitions as windows and beams were laid out on the street and auctioned off; some were used to renovate old city buildings, especially pubs, and what was left kept many a family in kindling through the winter.

The old buildings of St Peter's Street are long gone and the new City Hall is well under way while extensive works are being carried out on the site of the old municipal buildings to construct the new Market Place in the closing months of 1937.

The construction of the new City Hall, pictured here in full swing *c*.1938. The scaffolded clock tower is taking shape and the last remnants of St Peter's Street are being demolished. The full plans for the City Hall were never completed; behind the clock tower an incongruously blank wall faces up St Giles's Street where another wing was to extend to an even larger City Hall that would have completed a grand cloister of municipal buildings, but the winds of war were blowing and efforts in the late 1930s had to be diverted elsewhere.

The final touches, applied by the Italian craftsmen, draw the attention of small crowds as they complete the pavement of the new vista in front of City Hall in 1938. Deciding to go with what they had already achieved with a new City Hall, Fire Station, War Memorial Gardens and Market Place, the council saw this municipal complex opened by George VI and Queen Elizabeth on Saturday 29 October 1938.

Civic leaders, officials and civic office holders of Norwich pictured outside the Guildhall on Lord Mayor's Day, 1936. The men on the front row, from the left, are Deputy Lord Mayor Sir E. White, City Sheriff Captain D. Buxton and Lord Mayor Herbert Frazer. To the Lord Mayor's right is his wife, City Councillor Mrs Maud Frazer; it was the first time that the Lord and Lady Mayoress of Norwich were both serving councillors. Frazer was a popular local man; born in Calvert Street, he was educated at St Augustine's School. He worked at Howlett & White's shoe factory before becoming a full-time union official in 1926. Holding many civic offices, he worked tirelessly for Norwich, work recognised by the award of a CBE in 1973. For many years the city's oldest surviving Lord Mayor, he died in 1975.

The Lord Mayor, Sheriff, civic officials, sword and mace bearers on the steps of Norwich City Hall in 1977. The office of mayor in Norwich may be traced back to the 1404 Royal Charter that granted the city the right to have its own mayor, two sheriffs and 24 alderman who were elected for life. The title of mayor was doggedly preserved in the city until the 20th century. The last mayor, antiquarian Walter Rye, always maintained: 'The old plain Mayoralty of Norwich was more honourable than a later-given Lord Mayorship.' The city's first Lord Mayor, Mr E.E. Blyth, was appointed after Mr Rye completed his term of office in 1909. Norwich still enjoys the annual appointment of a Lord Mayor today.

A bustling Gentleman's Walk, March 1957. Unlike its neighbour, Rampant Horse Street, the Walk and the Market Place remained largely undamaged throughout the bombing of World War Two. Many of the shops retain their Georgian and Regency façades. Sadly the same cannot be said of the shop fronts at street level which were mostly 'modernised' with large plate glass windows and fittings which are so indicative of the 1950s and '60s. In the Norwich city plan of 1946 such changes would have been much in keeping with the large 'open plaza' which threatened to destroy what character the Haymarket and Gentleman's Walk had left – luckily the plan was not enacted – some plans really are best left on the shelf.

The bustling market *c*.1948. With Britain still enduring rationing on many products, the market in post-war Norwich was an ideal place to get a little more value for your coupons. Admittedly 'wide boys' would occasionally emerge with their beaten-up brown cases offering the more luxurious goods but most day to day items could be obtained here at reasonable prices. Many stalls entered into the spirit of 'make do and mend' selling second-hand clothing for all the family. And after a hard mornings shopping what better way to spoil yourself than with a creamy Aldous ice from the motorcycle van?

The tea and refreshment stall, Norwich market, November 1956. One of the distinguishing features of the market, even today, is its smells; the leather from the baggage stalls, the aromas of the fish and meat stalls, the sweet, clean smell of the linens and, most tempting of all, the smell of sizzling bacon from the refreshment stalls. From before sun-up the boilers were fired to serve tea and snacks throughout the working day for stallholders and customers alike.

The junction of the Walk, White Lion Street and the Haymarket c.1937. Seen here are Frederick Amies hairdressers, Lambert's tobacconists and the affectionately remembered Fifty Shilling Tailors which later became John Collier, 'The Window to Watch'.

Hosing down the Market Place *c.*1938. Centre of the picture, looking a little stranded, is the Sir Garnet Wolsey pub. At the turn of the last century it was just one of three adjoining pubs; the Half Moon, the Punch Bowl and Sir Garnet Wolsey which rounded the corner of Pudding Lane into the Market Place. It was truly a remarkable survival from the Market Place redevelopment of the 1930s. On the right can be seen the 'Tin Hut', headquarters of Norwich City Police 1911-38.

Gentleman's Walk looking towards the Haymarket when this first experiment in pedestrianisation of the area was enacted in May 1970. On the corner of White Lion Street can be seen the new John Collier store, Lamberts (with their blind down) were still going strong as the city centre tobacconist. Complete with their modernised shop fronts True-Form and Swears and Wells were just two of the fashionable footwear and clothing outlets on the Walk at the time. Finally dear old Millets for sturdy clothes, anoraks and providers of webbing lunch bags for generations of Norwich workers.

The magnificent frontage of Backs on the Haymarket *c.*1963. Known in the 19th century as a grocers, tea dealers, wine, spirit and hop merchants, they will be best remembered from the 20th century by their reputation as the finest vintners in the city. In their 600-year-old wine cellars they did their own bottling of beer and fine French wine.

A sight which will bring many nostalgic memories back to the social drinkers of Norwich – the lost and much lamented 'long bar' in Backs on the Haymarket *c.*1963. Here one could sip Norwich Silk Sherry and select the spices to have your wine mulled before your eyes in an antique copper double saucepan. Not considered in keeping with modern bars of the late 1960s, poor old Backs closed in 1971. The long bar was shortened and moved to a city night club and the exceptional cellars emptied of their barrels ending a family tradition which had been on the same premises for eight generations.

A wet day on the Haymarket, February 1967. These new shops really do show off what could have happened to more of Norwich under the 1946 city plan.

Lambert's Corner on the Haymarket August 1976. This was the place in the city to buy quality loose teas and coffee. For children it was a place of a multitude of rich smells and fascination. Mum would select the coffee beans and then they would be passed through the grinding machine and bagged up – it was magic. This was also the place to buy special chocolate and all manner of jams and preserves. Sadly, Lambert's are no more and although there are many quality shops in the city nowhere quite smells like the 'Mecca'.

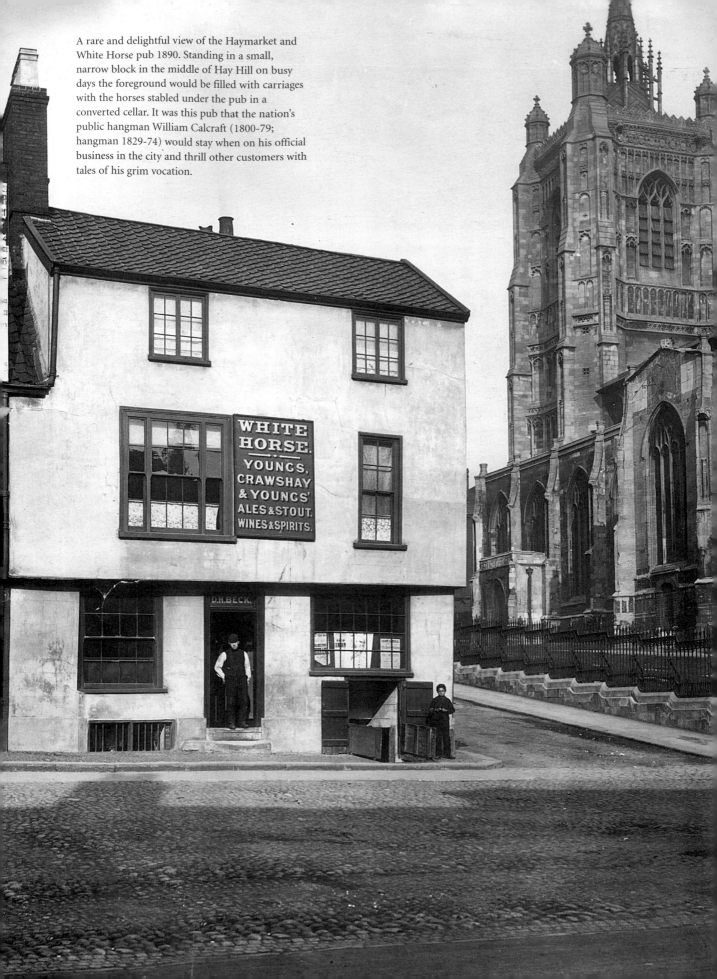

A rare and delightful view of the Haymarket and White Horse pub 1890. Standing in a small, narrow block in the middle of Hay Hill on busy days the foreground would be filled with carriages with the horses stabled under the pub in a converted cellar. It was this pub that the nation's public hangman William Calcraft (1800-79; hangman 1829-74) would stay when on his official business in the city and thrill other customers with tales of his grim vocation.

WHITE
HORSE.
YOUNGS,
CRAWSHAY
& YOUNGS'
ALES & STOUT.
WINES & SPIRITS.

Ceremony of the unveiling of the Sir Thomas Browne statue on Hay Hill by Lord Avebury on 19 October 1905. This event marked the tercentenary of Sir Thomas's birth in 1605. He was one of Norfolk's foremost writers and scholars in his day. An accomplished physician he wrote a classic analysis and defence of his profession in *Religio Medici* and contemplated the ancient cremations found in the county in *Hydriotaphia or Urne-Buriall*. Knighted by King Charles II at St Andrew's Hall, he died in 1682 and was buried in the nearby St Peter Mancroft Church.

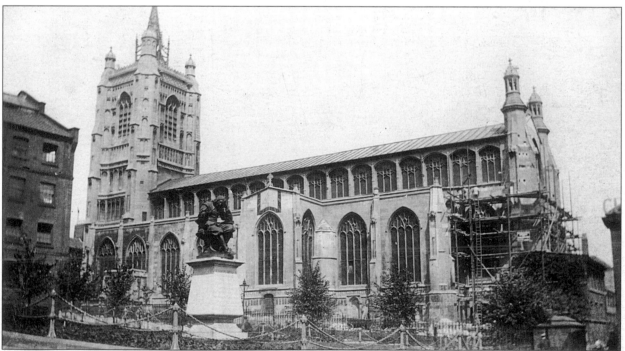

Hay Hill pictured *c.*1909. The background is dominated by St Peter Mancroft Church, with scaffolding around the east end for the restoration work to the masonry. Sir Thomas Browne's statue is surrounded by a small enclosed green, itself sadly swept away in the late 1960s in favour of a concrete plaza featuring fountains and pools. For most of their existence these were the focus of practical jokers who, amongst other pranks, squirted washing-up liquid into the jets to make them froth up. The water features were also removed and today the area is entirely concreted with steps down to the Haymarket. Sir Thomas remains – I wonder what he would make of it all.

From the Haymarket this *c*.1925 view looks down through Little Orford Street, while the tight corner branching off to the right is Brigg Street. There were many changes here throughout the 20th century. Burlington Buildings on the left, mostly occupied by International Stores, took the place of a fine Georgian-fronted bank demolished to make way for the trams in 1900. On the right may be seen Lipton's grocery store, now long gone and occupied today by a modern clothes store, while Chamberlain's and the Church of England Young Men's Christian Association building, severely damaged in the 1942 blitz, were replaced with the extended Curls (now Debenham's) and Pilch sports outfitters.

Brigg Street, 1957. Since the rebuilds after World War Two, little has structurally changed here although the same cannot be said about the businesses. When this photograph was taken Brigg Street was still open to two-way traffic and the well remembered shops in this area included Curls store, Hepworth's and Green's outfitters, Boots the Chemist, International Stores grocers and Pank's Radio. Today this area is pedestrianised and the aforementioned shops are all gone and replaced by high street jewellers, travel agents and fashion boutiques.

Back of the Inns to London Street

The Royal Arcade entrance from the Back of the Inns, 1958. Dating from 1899 the majority of this magnificent Art Nouveau frontage is still intact and in an apparent good state of repair. Designed and built by notable Norwich architect George Skipper on the site of the Royal Hotel, named so in honour of Queen Victoria's marriage in 1840, hence the name rather than 'title' of Royal Arcade.

Interior of the Royal Arcade
shortly after its opening in 1899.
Seen here on the right are the shops of Benjamin Bullen,
watchmaker; Emma Hurrell, florist; Lambert's tobacconist;
John Hallam the art dealer; Garland's drapers; Shapley & Co,
confectioners; Walter Boston, bootmaker and factor; Restieaux &
Co, stockbrokers; and Melia, Daniel & Co, grocers. One of the
most notable features of the arcade within living memory
was the picture of Christ in an art shop window which,
after lengthy observation, gave the illusion that the closed
eyes of Christ opened.

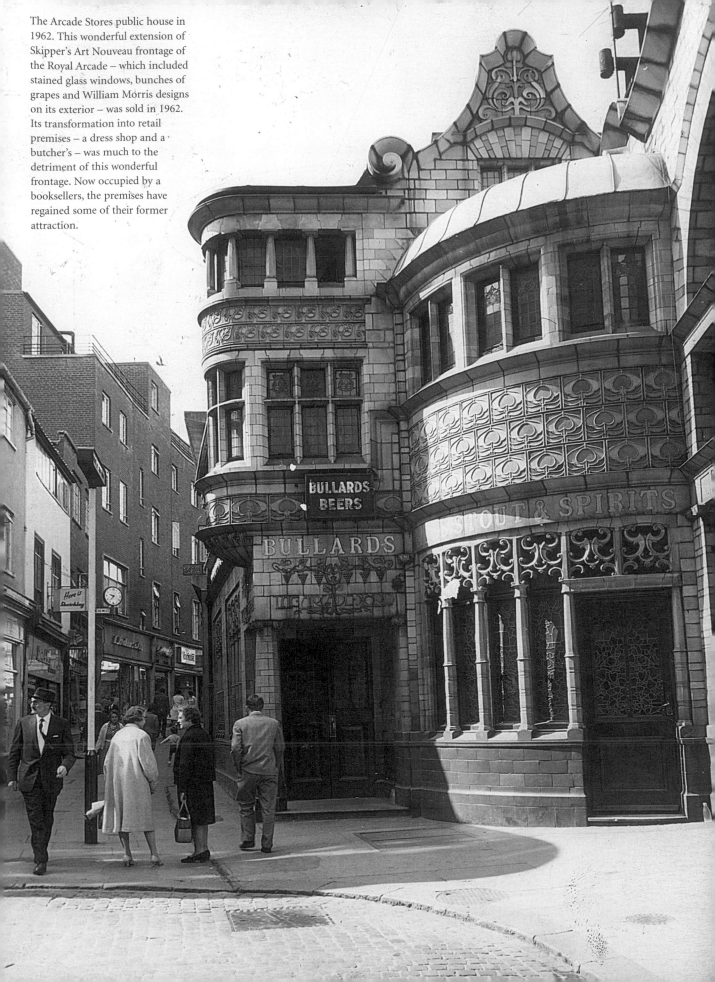

The Arcade Stores public house in 1962. This wonderful extension of Skipper's Art Nouveau frontage of the Royal Arcade – which included stained glass windows, bunches of grapes and William Morris designs on its exterior – was sold in 1962. Its transformation into retail premises – a dress shop and a butcher's – was much to the detriment of this wonderful frontage. Now occupied by a booksellers, the premises have regained some of their former attraction.

White Lion Street pictured in 1970 shortly before the street was closed to traffic in the city centre pedestrianisation experiment of the same year. Today the experiment has become a permanent fixture and the area resurfaced accordingly. Since the coming of the Castle Mall this street has undergone a great regeneration with shop fronts smartened up and new, diverse businesses coming to the area. During the 19th century this area was one of the ends of an area nicknamed Blood and Guts Alley which extended up Timber Hill to Ber Street. A haunt of the local soldiery, the White Lion pub (curiously nicknamed the Blue Monkey) – from which the street takes its name – was also another meeting place for the city's notorious Hell Fire Club.

Queue for Christmas meat at Craske's butchers on the junction of Back of the Inns and White Lion Street 1971.

Davey Place, 1962. In 1813 Alderman Jonathan Davey shocked the Guildhall Council Chamber by declaring, 'Gentlemen, I mean to put a hole in the King's head!' His refusal to withdraw or explain caused great concern, to such an extent that local constables were ordered to observe his movements. The following week, an inn was sold on the Walk, purchased by Alderman Davey. Demolition began the following day and a huge hole appeared in the façade of the King's Head pub! Turned into a 'shoppers' footstreet' Davey Place remains testimony to the good alderman's sense of humour – or was it his flair for publicity?

Back of the Inns and London Street have rung to many tunes (good and bad) from the city's array of buskers. Seen here on Davey Place corner in 1985, Steven 'Smiffy' Baker, the city's own 'pied piper', entertains with pipe and puppets. The children are (left to right): Kate Hockridge (three), Sara Wignall (three), Christopher Spillman (two) and, in his pushchair, little Gary Zipfel, aged one.

The policeman is on point duty and bunting is out in fine array on London Street, viewed from Jarrold's Corner, to commemorate the visit to the city of King George V on 28 June 1911, his first official visit to the city as monarch.

The bottom of Guildhall Hill, Jarrold's Corner and London Street with the decorations out for the coronation celebrations of HM Queen Elizabeth II in June 1953.

As many of the street-level shop fronts were modernised along the Walk from the Haymarket some of the last changes were enacted towards the Exchange Street/London Street areas. Seen here in 1962 dear old Hope Brothers' outfitters has held on to its old style while Burton's and Jarrold's dispensed with their inter-war frontages in favour of rounded columns and plate glass.

The grand frontage and final vestige of the Corn Exchange on Exchange Street pictured shortly before its demolition in 1964. The original Corn Hall was built in 1826, for £6,000, and was replaced in 1861 with a new, enlarged and grand-frontaged building constructed for £17,000. For just over 100 years agricultural trading, auctions and sporting events such as boxing and wrestling were hosted here. It was sold for redevelopment in 1963.

Pictured in 1961, trade is brisk in the Norwich Corn Exchange. All trading was carried out here under the portraits of Thomas William Coke, the Norfolk farming improver and MP and John Culley Esq, founder of the Corn Hall.

The unique atmosphere of the Wednesday auction at the Corn Exchange, August 1950. City women would come in their best hats and warm coats and, armed with flasks and sandwiches, settle around the auction tables for the day, looking for bargains, knick-knacks and things for the home, especially 'glass with a good ring or a nice bit o' china'. The men, many of them dealers who would have dusty side-street premises where they sold and delivered wardrobes and other furniture, wore hats that seemed glued to their heads while they passed the time bidding by 'hat tip or lug pull', smoking Woodbines, roll-ups or pipes.

London Street looking towards the Guildhall *c.*1925. Up to the late 19th century this section of London Street was almost an extension of the market. Barrow boys and street sellers congregated in this area. 'Windmills for jam jars', was a common cry met by children clustering around the gaily decorated barrow to exchange their old jars for the pretty toys. Here were watercress sellers, lavender sellers, muffin and pie men. Horses filled the area towing trade wagons and drays vying for space along with the gentry's carriages and thoroughbreds along the way. Here, as now, a few street entertainers gathered to perfom. Most endearing in the past was the girl who sang *Holy City* and *Star of Bethlehem* to the strains of a barrel organ outside the *Mercury* offices.

The fire at Garland's store, 1 August 1970. This terrible blaze began with a chip pan fire at 5pm. The alarm went out and tenders from Bethel Street fire station were soon on the scene, indeed, there were soon tenders from all over the locality that fought to contain the fire in this historic area of the city. It took over three hours to get the blaze under control.

After the horrific fire it took three years of reconstruction and refurbishment before Garland's could open for business again. Sadly the business never really recovered and announced its closure in January 1984. Today the department store houses several individual businesses which carry on similar trade, selling quality clothes, footwear and furnishings.

London Street *c*.1903. This street was but a quiet lane, known as Cockey Lane after the cockey or stream which ran along its length. During the 19th century it grew in importance as an entrance street to the city from the railway and was widened in 1857 and again in 1885. These improvements were not without casualties which included the house of John Bassingham, a member of the Goldsmith's Company, whose magnificent doorway is now incorporated into an entrance for the Guildhall. The other loss was the shop known as 'John of Allsorts' which was eventually replaced by the white-faced bank pictured to the right of the photograph.

Langford's the caterers of 50 London Street, established in 1872 and photographed here *c.*1934. The proprietor of Langford's since 1922 was one Ermino William Louis Marchesi, who in the absence of a speaker at Norwich Rotary Club, gave an address in which he declared the need for a club where young men could gather, exchange ideas, think and work on their own. Eager discussion followed in the coffee room of Langford's and, on 14 March 1927, a meeting was held at Suckling House where it was resolved to establish such a club. The name of that club was the Round Table, now an international organisation with active branches in 28 countries and still going strong!

The frontage of Miller & Co tobacconists, 37 London Street, photographed in 1977. It is best remembered for the magnificent lifesize and lifelike painted figure of an officer of the 42nd Regiment, 'the Black Watch', who stood an almost unbroken guard at the door for 170 years. The shop was founded by Mr Miller in 1812 and closed in September 1982. Sadly, the whereabouts of this great Norwich 'character' is not known today despite newspapers appeals and a lot of amateur detective work.

A bustling and unusual view of London Street in the 1930s with traffic not just flowing one way but in both directions. For those who remember old Norwich, two-way traffic on London Street is buried in the back of living memory. Those of us who remember the late 1960s and '70s and the Norwich City pedestrianisation experiments find it hard to conceive any other traffic than people using this area – especially on a Saturday morning when this packs full of people as one of the main shopping thoroughfares of the city.

London Street, 2002. A few modern shop frontages have crept in and certainly most of the businesses have changed, but look up and see how the strong Regency and Baroque-style frontages of the 19th century are still there and well maintained. People still throng London Street, the buskers play, depending on the season roast chestnuts or ice-creams are sold from handcarts, and fresh flowers are sold by the side of the pavement – some things really don't change.

Still a familiar feature on London Street today as Natwest, this photograph shows it when it was the newly built National Provincial Bank in 1924. The bank carried on a tradition of improvement of London Street that began in the 18th century and reflects the attempts of the provincial city to establish a street of 'London quality' business premises. Until 1922 the area this bank now covers was occupied by Henry Ash the Draper, The Domestic Bazaar Co Ltd and Mealing Mills auctioneers.

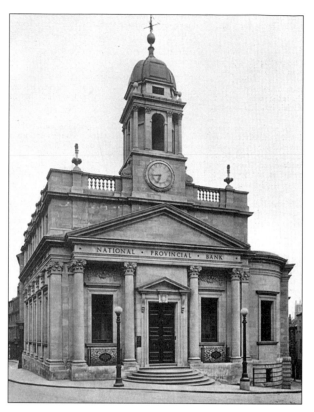

The famous W.E. Hovell's basket and wickerware shop on the corner of Bedford Street and Bridewell Alley, pictured in 1970. That year Miss D. Hovell sold the family business to Butchers under the condition they continued to trade under the name of Hovell's. The Hovell family had been in the basket trade in Norwich for about 200 years and had traded from this shop since 1864. Most of their materials were locally grown on the three acres of osier beds they had at the end of Cooper Lane in Old Lakenham. When W.E. Hovell took over the firm from his father in the late 19th century he expanded the business to two workshops and employed a total of about 30 men making everything from simple wicker baskets to beautiful suites of furniture which was exhibited at international exhibitions. After his death in 1955 his daughter took over the business which, although not in family hands, carries on many of the fine traditions of the old business today.

REDWELL STREET AND PRINCE OF WALES ROAD TO CARROW BRIDGE

Laying tram tracks just off Agricultural Hall Plain, at the top of Upper King Street, c.1900.

Redwell Street *c.*1890. Named after the so-called 'Red Well' situated in the corner of St Michael at Plea churchyard from where the residents of this area could draw their water until the city sanitation improvement of the late 19th century. In 1899-1900 half the buildings on the left were demolished to make way for the city's tram system.

Clearing the Redwell Street area for the new tram system *c.*1899. To the left of the photograph may be seen the tower of St Andrew's Church and, centre right, the Festival House pub. This new thoroughfare – which connected Castle Meadow, Bank Plain, St Andrew's and beyond – allowed quick and easy transport for workers in outlying districts of Norwich to factories in the city. Today it is hard to imagine this area without this cut, as the traffic speeds up the hill and on to Bank Plain.

Barclays Bank, Bank Plain, 1955. It was built in 1929 to the designs of E. Boardman on the site of a number of premises, including the old Bartlett Gurney Bank House. To many of the Norfolk farmers visiting Norwich on market day, this magnificent neo-Georgian edifice must have seemed like entering the portals of the Bank of England.

The Agricultural Hall, which gives its name to the Plain on which it stands, pictured about 1930 when hosting the second Eastern Evening News Homes Exhibition. Opened in 1882 by HRH the Prince of Wales, the Agricultural Hall was designed by city architect J.B. Pearce and used for all manner of exhibitions, public entertainments and livestock shows. Today it is part of the Anglia TV complex.

Prince of Wales Road, viewed from Agricultural Hall Plain c.1905. Then, as now, this area is one of the hubs of the city. Built to the form and grandeur we recognise today, Agricultural Hall Plain and Prince of Wales Road were to be the grand entrance boulevard to the city, crowned in this area by the Royal Hotel. The Royal opened in 1897 and the Bath stone Harvey's Bank on the right opened in 1866. Sadly, Harvey's Bank collapsed and for many years the building played host to the city's main Post Office. Today this building along with the Agricultural Hall make up the Headquarters of Anglia TV.

Prince of Wales Road, c.1950. A nostalgic view of this city vista familiar to visitors and residents, at this time Prince of Wales Road was predominantly an area of businesses and shops frequented by the employees of such as the railway, Bolton & Paul Engineering and Colman's Carrow Works travelling to and from work. In those austere post-war years, few folks had cars so the main mode of transport for the Norwich workforce was the bicycle. Prince of Wales Road used to look like Cambridge in term time – bicycles propped by shops, or queues of cyclists by the lights on the junction, waiting for the 'big push' to get started up the hill again. After a difficult decade or so following the closure of the riverside factories, Prince of Wales Road has been reinvented as an area of new offices, restaurants and nightspots.

A big delivery of Christmas stock to Willmott's cycle store on Prince of Wales Road, *c.*1930.

The new shop front of Wallace King's on Prince of Wales Road, 1950. Begun as an ironmongers in 1906 by Mr Wallace King, in a tiny lock-up shop in Upper Goat Lane, his business grew and by 1912 he had acquired new premises here at 24 and 26 Prince of Wales Road. Offering complete house furnishing, bedding and furniture manufacturers, picture frame makers and house removals, their premises extended a fair way behind and up St Faith's Lane. A kindly man known as a man 'long in the public eye but never in public life', he did much by small gestures of generosity for his customers. When he died, St Peter Mancroft Church overflowed. The business passed to his son and grandson, who proudly carried on the family tradition. They eventually had 10 stores across East Anglia but tragedy hit Wallace King Ltd when it was one of the casualties of the 1992 economic recession.

The Norwich Electric Theatre, 102-104 Prince of Wales Road shortly after it opened on 26 December 1912. This beautiful building was designed by Francis Burdett Ward and was the forerunner of many cinema designs. When 'talkies' came to this cinema in 1929, 89,000 people came to see *Sunny Side Up* during its five week run. Rechristened the Norvic in 1949, it lasted 12 more years until the majority of it was demolished in 1961.

The AA building and Prince of Wales Road during the floods of 26-28 August 1912. The streets here are crammed with curious spectators; on the deeper waterlogged areas carts and boats took visitors on tours for 1d a trip. When stock was taken of the damage across the county in the 1912 floods, it amounted to over £100,000, whilst 15,000 people lost homes or property.

Looking back up Prince of Wales Road from Foundry Bridge 1906. Prince of Wales road was built through the gardens of houses as a commercial speculation in the 1860s. In the distance can be seen the smart row of apartments known as Alexandra Mansions – the first residential flats in Norwich. The Mansions give a flavour of what the scheme set out to achieve. Sadly this project, which was intended to create a grand boulevard running from the station to the city, ran out of money halfway through and was never completed.

Winifred Brain standing beside the old newspaper and magazine stall familiar to thousands of Norwich commuters and visitors on the corner of Foundry Bridge near the station. The business had been run for 30 years by Mrs Brain's husband, Joe, and before that by his mother Mrs Edith Wright. This photograph dates from July 1973 when the old shed was pulled down in favour of the new outlet behind.

Thorpe Station *c*.1895. Opened in 1866, this distinctive station building with its zinc dome and fine French baronial façade was built by Young & Sons of Chapel Field Road. It replaced Norwich's first station which was situated just a short way downriver and opened in 1844 as the Norwich to Yarmouth line of the Eastern Counties Railway. Although trains have come and gone and transport has changed beyond imagination since this photograph was taken, this great station building has always been appreciated and has undergone several refits over the years to keep it in a good state of repair.

W.H. Smith's book and magazine stall on Thorpe Station, 1957. Although the grand station buildings have remained much the same since it opened in 1888, Thorpe Station has seen numerous refits and redesigns to its interior and surroundings throughout its existence. Today the station has been fully modernised, the platform centre shops which had been moved to the sides have been refitted as glass-fronted units, with an enquiry point taking their place platform centre.

A group of young trainspotters at Thorpe Station in 1954.

British Railways locomotive 4-4-0 at Thorpe Station, with driver, fireman, guard and station staff, 1956. Fifty years after the railways were nationalised, and nearly 40 years after the massive Beeching cuts, things turned full circle with the deregulation of British Rail into franchise and business-owned regional railways organised along similar lines to the railway companies of the 19th century.

The SS *Jenny Lind* stops off on her pleasure journey from Foundry Bridge, near the station to Thorpe Reach and Great Yarmouth, *c.*1909. Centre stage is the famous little Norwich character Billy Bluelight in his running gear. He is best remembered for racing alongside the boat, sometimes all the way to Yarmouth and back again. He greeted passengers as they left the boat – with his cap off to collect monetary appreciations for his feat. Still affectionately remembered in folk tales in the city and even in a pub name, 'Billy Bluelight', real name William Cullum, died on 10 July 1949 aged 90.

The Steam Packet Ferry 'quanting off' *c.*1885. Not driven by steam but taking its name from the pub where it was based on the opposite side of the river, this little ferry allowed folks to save a walk (and the expensive tolls on Carrow Bridge) between Foundry and Carrow Bridges by paying a 'copper' – a penny or ha'penny, depending on what you could spare – to cross the river to King Street. In the background are some of the malthouses of King Street, renowned for brewing at a time when there were three breweries, numerous malthouses and victuallers in this area of the city.

The River Wensum and the old Carrow Bridge with the wherry *Star of Hope* on the right *c.*1905. The factory buildings to the right are mostly occupied by the famous Norwich firm of J.J. Colman Ltd. Internationally famed for their mustard, the company diversified to many other products including Reckitt's Starch, Waverley Oats, Semolina and Almata (baby food). In the 1930s Carrow Works were the largest in Norwich – covering over 50 acres with almost a mile of river frontage – and employed 2,000 people.

HRH Edward, Prince of Wales (later Edward VIII) opening the new Carrow Bridge on 27 June 1923. Norwich City had one of the most pro-active corporations finding work for local men during the depression of the 1920s and 1930s. Great parks were laid out, public works, housing estates and a new city centre, including a City Hall were constructed. The Prince keenly supported these works and made no fewer than 11 visits to open completed projects during the inter-war years.

The trading vessel *River Ouse* passes through the opened Carrow Bridge, October 1950. The River Wensum has been navigated by trading craft since the earliest settlers came to what was to become the city of Norwich. It was only in the early 19th century that the route was properly organised under the Norwich and Lowestoft Navigation which, on its opening in September 1833, proudly proclaimed Norwich to be a port. Sadly, its great plans were never quite fulfilled, especially with the coming of the railways. Only the Clarence Harbour pub built near the station, where the docks were to have been built, bares witness to these high hopes.

RIVERSIDE TO PALACE PLAIN

Foundry Bridge, the Great Eastern Hotel and the yacht station on the Wensum near the station *c.*1950. The yacht station was opened in 1934 to offer holiday craft and day trippers a safe mooring while exploring the local waterways. In its first season, the vessels which used the facility numbered 573 and brought 2,600 visitors to the city. Since then the yacht station has been extended and is still a useful and bustling mooring in holiday season today.

Fanum House, on the corner of Riverside Road and Thorpe Road by the station, was the local headquarters of the Automobile Association. The AA moved here from Prince of Wales Road shortly after World War One. Pictured here about 1935, today the premises are almost entirely occupied by Sasses Restaurant.

The River Wensum viewed from Foundry Bridge *c*.1938. On the right is the yacht station opened a few years before in 1934 while in the distance the enigmatic monolith is the full gas holder of the Bishop Bridge Gas Works. On the left is the Riverside frontage of James Porter & Son timber merchants whose roadside entrance was on Recorder Road, with another wood yard at St George's in the city and another at Great Yarmouth. This area is now taken by smart new riverside apartments.

One of Norwich's most famous landmarks; Pull's Ferry. A 15th-century watergate, it straddled the water course that ran under its great arch to the Cathedral Close. After the water course was filled in during the 18th century, the gatehouse fell into ruin and was described in the 1869 history as the 'Roughest bit of picturesque in the city'. The ferry took its name from John Pull the landlord of the adjacent Ferry Inn and ferry keeper in 1769 and is seen photographed in the last full year of its operation in 1929.

A very rare engraving of the spring near Bishop's Bridge c.1798. The structure over the well bears the arms of the Pettus family and marks its erection by Sir John Pettus in 1608, when he was mayor of the city. A benevolent man who did much public good he had also erected the fish stalls by Fybridge the previous year.

Bishop's Bridge and its fortified barbican, drawn by Ninham in 1791. An ancient water crossing, the bridge we know today dates from 1257 and was fortified to form part of the city defensive walls in about 1345. Due to its close proximity to church lands, properties and the cathedral, it was maintained by the bishop until 1393. In 1549, despite the gates being newly reinforced, they stood as little defence when Kett and his rebels stormed the city from Mousehold. It was also from this gate that some of the dismembered body parts of the same rebels were displayed after the rebellion was put down. In 1791, the defensive barbican was removed, along with city walls and the majority of gates, leaving the bridge unadorned, as it would have looked when built in the 13th century.

An attractive early photograph of Bishop's Bridge c.1880. This 13th-century bridge is one of the oldest in the kingdom. There has probably been a river crossing here for almost 2,000 years since the Roman road, which crosses the modern-day city from east to west (St Benedict's Street to Bishopgate) spans the river here. Today the bridge is being preserved for the future, having been closed to cars and lorries since the 1990s.

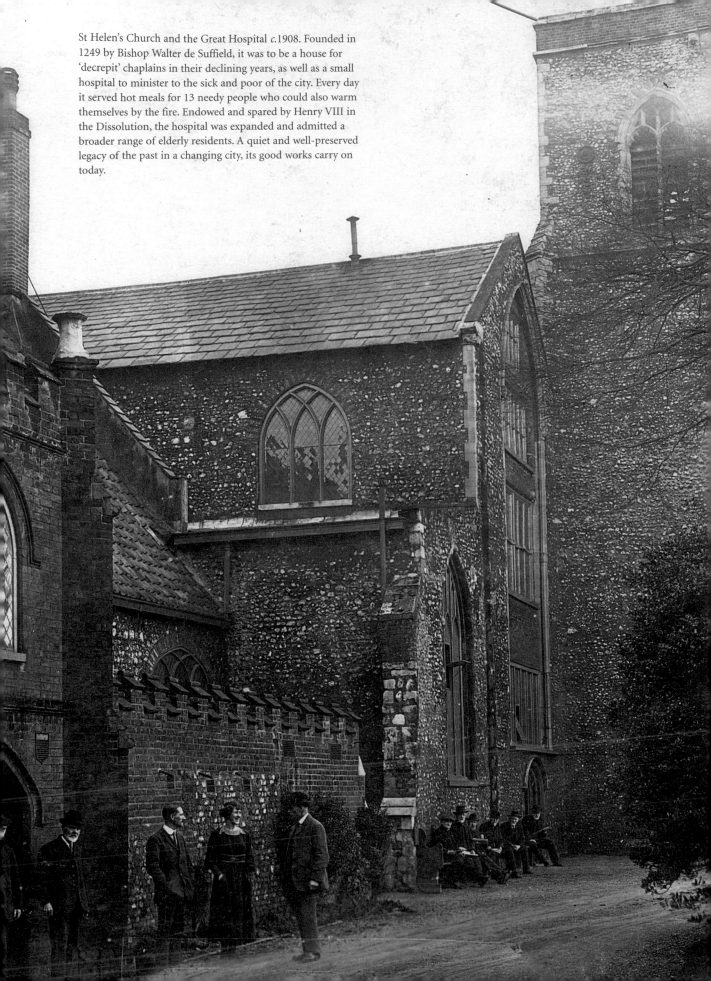

St Helen's Church and the Great Hospital *c.*1908. Founded in 1249 by Bishop Walter de Suffield, it was to be a house for 'decrepit' chaplains in their declining years, as well as a small hospital to minister to the sick and poor of the city. Every day it served hot meals for 13 needy people who could also warm themselves by the fire. Endowed and spared by Henry VIII in the Dissolution, the hospital was expanded and admitted a broader range of elderly residents. A quiet and well-preserved legacy of the past in a changing city, its good works carry on today.

Kett's Hill pictured *c.*1908. It derives its name from Robert Kett, who in 1549 led the local rebellion against enclosures and common rights. It is said that down this very hill Kett marched his army from their encampment on Mousehold to storm the city through Bishopgate. Apart from what proved to be a brief rebellion, this remained a quiet dusty little road until the mid-19th century when it became part of the new artisan suburb of the city known as Thorpe Hamlet. Today the road thunders with the riotous noise of traffic storming the city in rush hour.

Mousehold Heath and one of its commanding views over the city of Norwich 1957. Covering about 180 acres, Mousehold Heath, with its undulating heathland and woods, has provided a place of peace and recreation for generations of city dwellers. It proved inspirational to many artists and writers, notably the Norwich School, who recorded it well, and George Borrow, who eulogised its views in his recollections. For most city folks however it was an escape from the bustling city on a tupp'ny tram to 'Muzzle' or 'Mowsel' Heath.

Britannia Barracks *c.*1910. This familiar sentinel, which guards the Norwich skyline, was built in 1887 by the city corporation and given, as a mark of respect, to the Norfolk Regiment for its depot. Sadly, army reforms saw the amalgamation of the dear old Royal Norfolks in 1959 and the barracks were gradually taken over by the prison and private occupation, and finally lost its last ties to the military in December 1994 when the Regimental HQ of the Royal Anglian and Royal Norfolk Regiment Association moved to Aylsham Road.

Past glories; Sir Edmund Bacon, Lord Lieutenant takes the salute at the passing out parade of recruits after six weeks initial training at Britannia Barracks on 28 May 1952. Over the years of National Service thousands of young soldiers passed over these parade grounds and through the barracks gate on marches and manouevres over Mousehold. Good or bad they are all left with memories and nostalgia of those times, among them undoubtedly memories of the last depot Regimental Sergeant Major Bert 'Winkie' Fitt DCM.

The 19th-century refreshment pavilion on Mousehold Heath, resplendent after its renovation in 1964. Although the building is still well kept, it is today a popular burger restaurant. Sadly, the ornamental gardens have now gone and have been replaced with a grassy embankment easy to maintain. I must not be too critical though – it is still a lovely green place to enjoy an al fresco meal on a sunny day – an undoubted treat I have enjoyed many times since I was a lad.

The Cavalry Barracks (known from the 1920s as Nelson Barracks) viewed from Mousehold Heath c.1913. Erected on the site of the old manor house known as 'Hassett's Hall' between 1791 and 1793, it hosted just about every unit of British Regular Army Hussars, Dragoons and Lancers imaginable. This was something of which the city of Norwich was very proud and in its annual almanac it published a list of regiments stationed in the Cavalry Barracks from its inception. Demolished in 1965, today this area is mostly covered by council flats and houses.

Aerial view of Steward & Patteson's Pockthorpe Brewery, Barrack Street, 1921. Around it may be seen Silver Road, Mousehold Street, Anchor Street, and, in the top left, Mousehold Avenue and Ketts Cave. This whole area of terraced houses, short rows of shops, pubs and Nonconformist chapels was a community in its own right, most of its residents being employed in some capacity within the brewery and nearby shoe factories. As the brewing industry became increasingly mechanised, fewer people worked there and with its eventual closure in 1970, not only did the city lose its oldest extant brewery, but with it also ended a way of life for a whole community.

Close up view of the Steward & Patteson's brewery buildings, proudly displaying their royal warrants above the door, Barrack Street, November 1963. This business could trace its roots back to 1793 when John Patteson bought a small brewery in Pockthorpe from Charles Greeves. Under John Patteson the business rapidly expanded and, within five years, production had almost trebled. Joined by the Steward brothers in the early 19th century, it was to be a powerful allegiance which saw the brewery's expansion over a considerable area of Pockthorpe in the 19th century. After buying a number of the old established Norwich breweries, S & P were themselves bought out by Watney's in the late 1960s. The last brew was prepared here in 1970 and the old brewery completely demolished by 1974. Today the site is occupied by residential housing and offices.

Barrack Street *c.*1920, showing its distinctive blend of timber-framed Tudor houses and Victorian terraces before the slum clearances of 1921 and 1937. The community here knew hard times and local legend recalls their reliance on used tea leaves and beer-soaked bread. The vicar of St James's Church, speaking in 1880, made particular note of street brawls 'which certainly would not be tolerated elsewhere in the city; this parish is to Norwich what Seven Dials or Bethnal Green are or were to London.'

The Yarn Factory Tavern on the corner of Cowgate Street and Fishergate *c.*1948. Demolitions of the late 1960s and the creation of the inner city link road has changed this area beyond all recognition.

Thoroughfare Yard, which connects Fishergate with Magdalen Street, *c.*1920. Few of these yards remain today because, rather than them being the charming old buildings from the sketches and photographs of the past, they were in fact slums. Even in the 20th century, the living conditions were cramped, often damp, and many such dwellings had no sanitation of any description. The disease and misery they harboured outweighed any claim that these crumbling tenements had beauty or charm. Most of these were demolished in the 1920s and '30s and the people rehoused in the council flats and houses across the city, and at Mile Cross (the country's first council housing estate), constructed at the same time.

Quay Side and the river viewed from Fye Bridge, *c.*1900. This area of the riverbank has a Flemish flavour consisting of Pigg Lane and Bedding Lane leading back to St Martin's at Palace Street. In mediaeval times this was probably the busiest part of the river in the city. Trading vessels would have lined the moorings and the lanes bustled with carts. This photograph shows the last remnants of that great trade and although having weathered indifferent fortunes in the late 20th century, this area is today undergoing restoration as an attractive residential area.

St Martin at Palace Plain, 1957, so named after the church of St Martin at Palace seen to the right of the photograph. Frazer's joinery and the old Palace gas works, which spread behind and beside the church, were demolished in the 1970s and here now are the city's new Crown Courts, opened in November 1988.

KING STREET AND MAGDALEN STREET TO ANGLIA SQUARE

Exterior approach to the King Street Gate in 1792, drawn by Henry Ninham. Also known as Conesford Gate, this gate was connected by the city wall to the boom towers which were situated on either side of the River Wensum; fitted with winding gear and a chain of Spanish iron drawn between them, they 'policed' the river traffic, while the King Street Gate provided protection for this valuable trading area from undesirables on the road. Under 'City Improvements' with threats of the complete levelling of the old city walls between 1791 and 1810, King Street Gate was torn down but large ruinous remnants of city wall, towers and defences may still be found in this area today.

Repairing part of the ancient city wall near King's Street, *c.*1950. This picture shows the ruined tower near Cinder Ovens Row and in the background, up the wooded hill towards Bracondale, the 'Black Tower' otherwise known as 'Duke of Buckinghamshire's Tower' and 'the Snuff Tower'. This tower was preserved with a thatched roof until 7 July 1833 when 'a fireball about the size of a man's head', fell upon the thatched roof and burnt the tower out.

The Music House, King's Street, *c.*1950. Reputedly the oldest house in Norwich, it was built around 1175 by the Jurnets, one of the wealthiest Jewish families in England. It was one of the town houses of the Paston family in the 16th century, from whom it passed to Sir Edward Coke, Chief Justice to Elizabeth I. The Music House was headquarters of the Norwich waits or minstrels, established in the reign of Elizabeth I, hence the name which was retained when, in the 19th century, Youngs, Crawshay and Youngs owned it as an inn. It now belongs to Norfolk County Council and is known as Wensum Lodge.

A drover and two head of cattle on King's Street *c*.1925. One of the oldest streets in Norwich, it was here that the Saxons made their settlement, which became known as Conesford, beside the old Roman marching route which ran from near Carrow Bridge, along King's Street to near Fye Bridge. During the 19th century this street was predominantly occupied by breweries, malthouses and over 43 pubs and beer houses.

A nostalgic view of the inside of Norwich City Lads' Club in March 1953. Founded thanks to the efforts of a chief constable of Norwich, J.H. Dain, it was formally opened by HRH Prince Henry, Duke of Gloucester, on 2 June 1925. Generations of city boys came to the club to take part in organised activities, from gymnastics to St John Ambulance work. The club will, however, be best remembered for its strong tradition of boxing and its notable champions like Ginger Sadd and Herbie Hide. Alas, in the 1990s the lads' club closed its doors for the last time.

Upper King's Street *c.*1960. On the left is the Nag's Head pub, originally part of the old Norwich city Greyfriars priory. Opposite the Nag's Head is yet another pub, the Cock, and beside the Nag's was Mann, Egerton & Co, electrical engineers, and a short row of shops which included a tailor, tobacconist and butcher before King's Street is bisected by Rose Lane. This last row of shops has, after years of dilapidation, been transformed into a trendy set of offices known as St John's House.

A bustling Upper King's Street, seen from its junction with Prince of Wales Road *c.*1947. On the left may be seen part of the Gothic façade of the Royal Hotel while on the right the grand eastern branch offices of the Commercial Union Assurance Company Limited. Then, as now, this area was occupied predominantly by solicitors, auctioneers, estate agents and barristers.

Upper King's Street by the junction of Bank Street, 1960. On the left is Woolwich House, then city office of the Woolwich Equitable Building Society, well remembered for its military pargetting and distinctive weather vane of an artilleryman and his cannon. The other, most notable change is the old zebra crossing has now been replaced by a pelican crossing due to increased traffic in this area.

An unusual view of the stalls on the cobbles by Prince's Street and the Army and Navy Stores, Tombland c.1955. Among them are W.B. Howard, tobacconist, and the Tombland florist and fruiterer, and beyond that still, a small sweet stall. This was an attempt by Norwich Corporation to erect semi-permanent stalls here, which led to two High Court Actions in which a citizen, Mr Kent, fought the council and won, thus establishing for all time that Tombland was a permanent open space.

An early view from the 1880s looking across Tombland towards St George's Church from the Ethelbert Gate. Tombland derives its name from the Anglo-Saxon *tom lond*, which means 'open space'. This open space was the Market Place for the bordering settlements of Conesford, Westwic and Northwic, which grew to become the basis of the city of Norwich.

A quiet Tombland with tram and carriage for hire with cabby leaning beside, *c*.1905. The obelisk to the far right of the photograph was a public drinking fountain erected by John Henry Gurney in 1860. Near this site was the machinery used between 1700 and 1850 to raise and store water for the higher parts of the city.

Running behind St George's Church and connecting Prince's Street and Tombland is Tombland Alley, pictured here about 1910. To the left and over the archway, then in a poor state of repair, may be seen Augustine Steward's House. A wealthy merchant, he was mayor of Norwich in 1534, 1546 and 1556. Undoubtedly, his most turbulent period in office was in 1549 when, as deputy mayor, he had to take over from the mayor himself who had been taken prisoner and removed from the city walls by rebels during Kett's Rebellion. His remarkable house was partially restored after World War Two and became the city's tourist information centre; sympathetically restored in the 1990s, today it is an antiques centre.

The west front of Norwich Cathedral c.1950. It was begun in 1096 by Bishop Herbert de Lossinga, shortly after he moved the seat of the bishopric to the city from Thetford. Sadly he was not to see his new building finished; his successor Eborard completed the church by about 1140. The original spire, constructed from wood, was destroyed in the hurricane of 1362. It was replaced by the 315ft-high stone spire we know today, which was completed in 1480. Its roof bosses are some of the finest and most diverse in the world and have recently been restored. To celebrate the Millennium the niches either side of the great west door were filled, with the stone figures of St Benedict and Mother Julian.

Erpingham Gate *c*.1900. This was built in 1420, along with the choir stalls inside the cathedral, by Sir Thomas Erpingham, the loyal Norwich knight, who led the English archers at Agincourt in 1415, as a mark of thanksgiving for their victory. His kneeling figure, complete with snowy white hair and beard, with his sword by his side is believed to have once stood on his tomb inside the cathedral. Today it rests in the niche directly over the gateway.

A photograph from the early 1880s showing the Ethelbert Gate before its 20th-century restoration. Following altercations between the city and the cathedral priory, Norwich citizens' displeasure culminated in a mob attack on 9 August 1272, during which the Precinct Gate, the church of St Ethelbert inside it, the bell tower and most of the wooden buildings of the monastery were destroyed. The citizens were punished and heavily fined for this and later built the Ethelbert Gate as an act of reparation.

Samson and Hercules House *c*.1900. Built on the site of Sir John Fastolf's manor house by Christopher Jay to 'signalise his mayoralty of Norwich' in 1657. The famous figures were placed outside the door about 1789. The building was restored by its owner, noted antiquarian George Cubitt, at the end of the 19th century.

After becoming a YWCA in the 1920s, Samson and Hercules House was bought in 1934 by Teddy Bush, who developed the building into a ballroom, café-restaurant and swimming pool, seen here shortly after it opened in 1935. Described on advertising as 'the centre of Norfolk', for the last 50 years it has been solely used as a nightclub of various names. The figures of Samson and Hercules still stand guard either side of the door, although they are only replicas of the originals, which were removed for conservation purposes in 1993.

Tombland looking towards Wensum Street *c.*1903. The mock Tudor-fronted building directly in front of us is the Maid's Head Hotel; an inn with origins as far back as the 13th century, when it was known as the Molde Fishe Tavern, but by 1472 its name had changed to the Maid's Head. Many visits by significant people have been made here; it was visited by the Black Prince in 1359, by Cardinal Wolsey in 1520 and the King's Commanders had breakfast here on the morning of the last battle of Kett's Rebellion. Saved by Walter Rye, the noted Norfolk historian, from the threat of demolition at the turn of the last century, it was restored and remains one of the city's premier hotels.

Tombland looking down Wensum Street, with, on the right, the memorial to Nurse Edith Cavell, the heroine and martyr executed by Germans in October 1915. The photograph dates from *c.*1920, shortly after the memorial was unveiled. On the left may be seen the Wagon and Horses pub, said to be named to record a wager whereby 'Mad' Wyndham of Felbrigg Hall wagered he could drive a wagon and horses up the narrow Wagon and Horses Lane at speed without touching the sides, a wager he is said to have won. Since 1976 the pub has been known as the Louis Marchesi, named after the founder of the Round Table, whose first meeting was held in Norwich in 1927.

Seen here is Wensum Street *c.*1895. One of the shortest streets of the city, it runs from the Maid's Head Hotel to Quay Side. In 1890 one court (Flower's Court), one yard (Ribs of Beef Yard) and 22 businesses could be found along its short length. The businesses were quite diverse and they included W. Low and Co. hay and straw merchants, Charles Holborn decorators, William Henry Claxton herbalist and Jethro J. Rice stationer.

Wensum Street, 1899. In real contrast to the previous photograph this image, showing the laying of the new tram system, demonstrates that wholesale destruction of historical areas and buildings is nothing new. This is clearly shown where the road has been widened and has literally cut some of the buildings like George Edwards's family boot and shoemakers' shop in half.

Fye Bridge Street *c*.1899. Reputedly the shortest street in Norwich, it is situated between Wensum Street and just over Fye Bridge, finishing at St Clement's Alley. On the left of the photograph, just beyond H.J. Attwell's greengrocer and Guyett's boot makers, was the original Ribs of Beef pub, kept for many years in the 19th century by the Norwich pugilist John 'Licker' Pratt. After the road-widening scheme of the 1930s, these buildings were replaced by part of the bridge approach and the Fye Bridge Tavern (now itself known as the Ribs of Beef). The new Fye Bridge was opened for traffic on 1 July 1933.

Magdalen Street (left) and Fishergate (right) viewed from Fye Bridge *c*.1965. Around the corner are the offices and factory shop of Howlett & White Limited, a branch of the Norvic Shoe Co. Ltd. With factories at Norwich, Northampton and Mansfield, Howlett & White proudly claimed to be England's premier shoe manufacturer. They also boasted in the late 1930s that they were producing 2.5 million quality shoes each year.

Magdalen Street from Colegate Corner, March 1959. Probably looking the best it ever did in the 20th century, this shows Magdalen Street during its facelift – carried out with the help of Mr Duncan Sandys MP and the Civic Trust. The result was a tremendous success and made Norwich and Magdalen Street world famous. It showed that, with the careful restoration of decaying shop frontages, a street which had been in decline could be regenerated.

Looking up Magdalen Street from Stump Cross, with the junction of Botolph Street to the right, December 1967. In the 19th century Magdalen Street was a street of great contrasts; shops with elegant fronts and the beautiful homes of notable local families such as the Gurneys and Martineaus stood cheek-by-jowl with the dilapidated housing of the poor in the courts and yards which ran off the street.

The refit and resurface of the Magdalen Street end of Botolph Street near Stump Cross. This was part of the £90,000 civic improvement project for the Magdalen Street area regeneration in 1959.

The strong Georgian frontage of Barclays Bank at Stump Cross on the junction with Botolph Street (left) and Magdalen Street (right). In the improvements of 1959 this frontage was sympathetically painted, fitted for night-time illuminations and the intrusive signs removed. This worked very well and was an attractive improvement; the pity of it was that just over 10 years later this attractive little corner of the city was mercilessly wiped out to make way for a shopping precinct and a concrete flyover.

Magdalen Street, 2002. After the hard work and great hopes for Magdalen Street, some bright spark goes and puts a hideous inner link road flyover across it, thus wiping out history and charm to such an extent that the area is still reeling. Large sums of money have since been invested in improvements and regeneration; there are still some superb shops for fabrics or antiques and quality furniture. Even that endangered species, the secondhand record store, can be found here squeezed amongst charity shops. When looking back on the pre-flyover street, one cannot help but recall the adage of Mark Twain: 'If it ain't broke, don't fix it!'

The Magpie Road and Magdalen Street junction viewed from the Artichoke pub, 1964. An historic gate to the city stood here and the inns outside the walls did a great trade with travellers who found the city gates closed. It was this route which the mediaeval monks traverse, from the nearby Magdalen Hospital (from which much of the area derives its names) to their cells in the cathedral priory. When the road was widened here in the 1960s, the White Swan pub was demolished and this revealed a large section of the city wall which is still visible today.

Magdalen Road lined with onlookers while two packed trams pass by to celebrate the opening of operations of the Norwich city tramway on 30 July 1900.

The shops on Magpie Road, 1967. Situated in an area of terraced houses and close communities, this little row of small shops are remembered with affection by residents of the area. Many youngsters had their first bicycle bought for them from the second-hand bicycle shop. The garden shop is remembered for its aroma of fresh-cut chrysanthemums, its lovely greenery and the many buckets of water standing in the shop. Most memorable of all was the Cabin sweet shop and tobacconist where many a child was sent to get dad's fags on a Sunday.

Aylsham Road viewed from St Augustine's with Magpie Road to the right c.1905. This long and fairly straight road continues to the borough boundary and beyond. It existed as a lane for many years, but owes much to the turnpike which greatly improved the old trackway in the late 18th century. Initially, from 1874, a turnpike ran between between Norwich and Aylsham; a second leg running from Aylsham to Cromer was set up in 1811. This link did much for the early promotion of Cromer as a health resort, so much so it was described as '…the best of all the sea bathing places' in Jane Austen's *Emma* published in 1816.

Poor St Augustine's School, destroyed by a 500kg bomb dropped during the Baedeker Blitz on the night of 27-28 April 1942. Although the school had an air-raid shelter for children, and acted as a feeding centre for bombed-out families, no one was on the premises at the time and thankfully there were no injuries. After the war this bomb site was cleared and turned into a swimming pool which opened in 1961. In 1997 structural faults were found and, despite an active campaign, it was demolished and remains a development site today.

St Augustine's Street photographed in 1966 when it was described as having '…almost every commodity and service necessary in a modern community'. At the time St Augustine's Street had followed the lead of Magdalen Street and many of the shops had been modernised or renovated inside and out. There was great hope in the city at the time but, alas, this area has seen a sad decline over the last 20 years and is in need of considerable investment before its fortunes can be restored.

A very rare photograph of Botolph Street *c*.1910. The road takes its name from the church of St Botolph which stood on the north-east side of the street, near its junction with Magdalen Street. This church was sold after the Dissolution of the Monasteries in 1544 and was promptly demolished. An important link road between St Augustine's and Magdalen Streets, at the time this photograph was taken there were five pubs, 11 yards, 39 shops and businesses and a girls' home along its length. Today almost nothing remains, its place taken by Anglia Square shopping precinct and offices.

The construction of Anglia Square shopping precinct and the Odeon cinema, January 1971. This was prior to the building of the flyover and multi-storey office buildings later occupied by CCTA and HMSO. To the right of the picture can be seen the temporary road which was built to allow construction workers access to the upper deck.

At what cost to heritage was this built? Two listed buildings and the dolls' hospital fell for the flyover alone. Demolished for the main site was Botolph Street with its mix of buildings, some dating back to the Tudor period, with Regency, Victorian and Edwardian frontages. The village quality of this street was noted by Pevsner and summed up by John Howard in *Doors and Doorways of Old Norwich* in 1896. All destroyed in the wake of 1970s 'progress' – what vision!

Elm Hill to St Benedict's

A remnant of St Benedict's Gate, part of the city wall photographed about 1935 makes a fine frame for this this tranquil view of St Benedict's Street. What was to happen on the nights of 27-28 and 29-30 April 1942 could not be imagined in the worst nightmares of anyone around when this photograph was taken. This area was blown sky-high and reduced to a scene of total devastation, indeed it was considered one of the hardest hit in Norwich during the whole war. One resident of Grapes Hill recalled that he thought the end of the world had come.

Elm Hill c.1929. With hindsight it is inconceivable that, when this photograph was taken, Elm Hill was designated a slum and serious consideration was being given to the demolition of the whole area and its fate lay on the committee table of Norwich City Council. The vote was taken and Elm Hill was saved by one vote. Today Elm Hill is the uncontested jewel in the crown of Norwich's street heritage. Crammed with all manner of interesting shops selling crafts and collectables, it is visited by tourists from all over the world.

The gabled Pettus House, 41-43 Elm Hill, when kept by William Henry West, the scale maker (who also had premises at 41 Exchange Street) c.1922. At one time or another, between 1556 and 1776, nine mayors lived on Elm Hill. This house, but a fragment of the original great house which once spread down the hill to the church of SS Simon's & Jude's, was built by the Pettus family in the 16th century. A Norwich family traceable back to the 15th century, they provided generations of mayors and aldermen to the city, among them Sir John Pettus, mayor in 1608 and one of the few men ever to be sheriff of both city and county. The house stands today, now a very fine wine shop.

St Andrew's Hall *c.*1910. Built as a monastic building with a cloister for the Dominican or 'Black Friars' in the 13th century, it was forfeited to the Crown at the Dissolution. It was bought by the city – 'a fair and large hall for the Mayor and his brethren for assemblies for £81' with a further £152 wrung out of the city by the king's men to leave the lead on the roof! Still a magnificent venue in the city for concerts, conferences and antique fairs, since 1824 it has been home to the Norfolk & Norwich Music Festival.

The historic quarter of the city known as St George's Street. Previously known by a selection of names – including Blackfriars Bridge Street – it has been an important trading area since the earliest Saxon settlements. On the left of the photograph can be seen the factory which provided the major trade of boot and shoemaking. In 1868, Norvic – which began as Howlett & White's – opened what was claimed as the largest shoe factory in Britain. Closing in the early 1970s, this section on St George's Street remained gaunt and redundant, whilst the part of the factory which faced Colegate was converted into offices for the Norwich Union insurance company. In the 1980s speculators converted the empty section into the Atrium, a trendy shop and wine bar centre with offices above. Sadly the retail units were not successful and today the whole building is occupied by offices, but the wine bar remains.

Looking up St Andrew's Street *c*.1890. It is hard to imagine this narrow cobbled street becoming one of the busiest in the city less than 10 years after this image was captured. At that time, St Andrew's dog-legged to the left beside St Andrew's Plain and ran directly on to the road known today as Princes Street. Access to Redwell Street and Bank Plain was via the crossroads at the top of Elm Hill. This winding street arrangement was alleviated with the implementation of the Norwich tramway in 1899 when the City Arms pub was torn down, along with part of Redwell Street, to allow trams access directly up the hill from St Andrew's on to Bank Plain beside St Michael at Plea Church.

Looking down St Andrew's Street from the church wall towards Charing Cross *c*.1895. The little opening to the left, with a shop on the corner, is Bridewell Alley. The large building on the right, slightly set back from the street is the St Andrew's Steam Clothing & Hosiery Works of F.W. Harmer & Co, established in the city in 1826.

The burnt-out shell of F.W. Harmer's works on St Andrew's Street in 1943. Poor old Harmer's – doing their bit for the war effort, making all types of uniforms for civilian and military forces – were hit several times throughout the war. The grand old works were never rebuilt and the factory was relocated to a prefabricated building at Heigham where it remained until the 1990s when Harmers withdrew their interests in the city and closed the factory.

Stuart Hall and Suckling House, St Andrew's c.1920. According to the oval plaque high on the wall of Suckling House, the site has been in occupation since 1285 when William de Rollesby lived there. The house as we know it today is a Tudor rebuild and bears the name of its occupant at the time: Robert Suckling MP and mayor of the city in 1564. The house was restored in 1923 by Ethel and Mary Colman, members of the famous mustard family, and given to the city along with Stuart Hall (built as a memorial to their sister, Laura Elizabeth Stuart) in October 1925. Used for many years for public functions, meetings and presentations, the buildings today house a cinema and café.

Theatre de Luxe (colloquially pronounced as 'theatre de loo') on St Andrew's Street c.1947. Opened in 1910 this was the first building specifically designed for films, although its construction involved the conversion of former premises. Always a popular venue, it was enlarged in 1920 to seat 1,000 patrons. The last Norwich cinemas to convert to 'talkies' in 1931, it was the first to show 3D films in the 1950s. Audiences began to dwindle and Saturday matinees were seen more as sessions for pranks than watching films. The 'flea-pit' was closed in 1957 and demolished soon afterwards.

The Norwich Public Library at the corner of St Andrew's and Duke Streets opened in 1857. Expanded over the years, when this photograph was taken about 1922 it contained about 22,000 reference works, a local collection of 7,000 volumes, 8,000 pamphlets, 7,000 topographical prints and a junior library of over 4,000 books. Today all central Norwich libraries are housed in the Millennium Library, and this superb old building has been demolished to make way for a telephone exchange and multi-storey car park.

A very rare photograph of St John's Street (left), St John's Alley (right) and the church of St John Maddermarket c.1905. Right of centre may just be discerned one of the last parish pumps left in the city. The water from this pump was referred to as 'essence of the graveyard' and really wasn't much cleaner than the river. Of course, waterborne diseases were prevalent here and it is not surprising to learn that during the early 19th century Norwich had one of the highest infant mortality rates in the country.

Roman Catholic Chapel, St John's Alley *c.*1905. One of the oldest Roman Catholic chapels in England, it was erected in 1794, previous to which the congregation had attended the chapel in the Duke's Palace. In 1910 their new church of St John the Baptist was built on Earlham Road and for a few years the old chapel became a baking powder factory. In 1921 it was purchased by Nugent Monck as a home for the Norwich Players and still known today as the Maddermarket Theatre.

The Maddermarket Theatre, 1948. Nugent Monck raised the £3,000 for the venture from keen supporters and did a pretty good job of converting the interior of the old chapel into a copy of an Elizabethan theatre for the performance of Shakespeare. Now one of the most respected amateur companies in the country, the good work is carried on today with the players and visiting repertory companies, as well as theatrical workshops which makes the Maddermarket one of the most popular arts venues in the city.

One of the author's favourite views of the old city, this is a bustling Charing Cross *c.*1908. Its name is derived from the stone structure which stood between what is now the junction of St Andrew's Street and Duke Street and St John Maddermarket (removed in 1732; the same year the old market cross was taken down). Around this ancient cross was a small market which sold dyes to the weaving industry. One of the most sought after was the madder plant used in dye making and which gives a red tone – hence the Maddermarket.

This delightful photograph shows A.T. Clissold's outfitters at 16a Charing Cross *c.*1930. This little shop took up the St Benedict's side of the Pigeons pub, kept at the time by Mr F.R. Clark who maintained the pub's notable tradition of selling good beer at a fair price. These two buildings have now been combined and are now one big pub known as the Hog in Armour.

St Benedict's Street, July 1957. Much of St Benedict's, particularly in the area around 'the Gates' was devastated during the 1942 Baedeker Blitz. Pictured after its post-war rebuilding and judicious improvement scheme, we see it in its heyday as a 1950s shopping street. As more people shopped in the city centre, trade here dwindled and more specialist shops selling musical instruments, collectables and furnishings took their place. It is still a street of treasure and pleasure today.

The Scientific Anglian secondhand and antiquarian bookshop, situated in the old Walker's Stores grocer's shop at 30 St Benedict's Street, photographed in 1989. It was established in 1967 by the original Scientific Anglian himself, Norman Peake, expert geologist, authority on the city chalk mines and airships. His knowledge is wide and learnedly attained. I have heard him discuss, with authority and knowledge, topics as diverse as a bus being partially swallowed by a road collapse in Norwich to feline ailments. In 2002 a fire officer and a Norwich City Council safety officer found such faults with the premises, tragically Mr Peake was left with no alternative but to close his shop. The Scientific Anglian was more than a place of business – it was an experience the like of which we will not see again.

St Benedict's Street after its post-war refurbishment, photographed in July 1957. It seems the bombing tightened the resolve of Norwich folk to rebuild not only the damaged areas of the city around them, but also to carry on their old established businesses. On this photograph, shops like Green's outfitters at 42-44, and Walter Mace, the general draper at 50-56, could trace their shops back a few generations.

As general high street custom faded from St Benedict's Street, many of the long-established shops and firms closed for good. Into their empty premises went more specialist businesses; the mood of change in the area was typified by the opening of the Norwich Community Arts Centre in October 1977. Alas, despite the high hopes of its early years, it has fallen into decline and sadly closed in 2002.

St Swithin's Alley *c.*1935. This historic little corner of Norwich ran from the tower of St Swithin's Church and contained Hampshire Hog Yard, just off St Benedict's Street. The thatched cottages were saved from demolition in the mid-1930s and were restored. The gabled 16th-century houses were not so fortunate and were demolished under a slum clearance scheme in 1937.

The lower section of St Benedict's Street, near St Benedict's Gate *c.*1968. On the left is Henry Jarvis & Sons, drapers, resplendent in its post-war refit and well-decorated windows ready for Christmas. This large shop was founded in about 1910 by Henry Thomas Jarvis at number 55. When joined by his sons they expanded to sell house furnishings and opened a funeral business, gradually spreading to take over the neighbouring shop premises as their enterprise grew. Today the shops have gone back to single occupation business premises and no hint is left of the popular old Jarvis shop used by generations of folks from this part of the city.

One of the most famous and poignant images of the blitz on Norwich, this is the church of St Benedict's Street pictured the morning after it was almost totally destroyed during the Baedeker Blitz of 28-29 April 1942. Set back from the road, it is easily missed by passing tourists but its tower, all that remains of the historic church today, stands as a gaunt sentinel and a poignant reminder of the damage and loss of life inflicted on this area during World War Two.

Three ambulances and the patrol vehicles of the Norwich City Police Highways Department at their depot on Pottergate c.1931. The first police vehicles were bicycles supplied by Mr Kirby from his St Benedict's shop in 1911, and the first patrol cars were three BSA three-wheelers purchased in the early 1930s.

An unusual view of Pottergate from December 1964. In the top right corner the sign for the Bluebell pub, which stood at the bottom of Lower Goat Lane, is just discernable, while the porticoed top of the old Corn Exchange is just visible over the shop roofs in the middle distance. This rather dull area of dilapidated shops and dwellings has been regenerated in the last 30 years to become a popular area of specialist and high-quality shops.

Church House, Pottergate, 1983. As Pottergate enjoyed its regeneration in the 1970s and '80s, concerns were expressed as to the lengths Norwich City Council was taking with regard to its restoration. One critic recorded 'unfortunately the Corporation so often seems to either completely destroy a street by demolition, or kill it by kindness in the form of Walt Disney-ish renovations'.

Duke Street and Grapes Hill to Bethel Street

Carts and drivers line up for this now evocative advertising photograph for the Pearl Sanitary Steam Company Ltd of 199 Heigham Street in 1910. This area was renowned for its cleaning and washing activities, the air filled with the pungent aroma of the steam engines that drove the washing machines combined with that of hot, wet linen, soap flakes and starch. Just a short distance away was The Swan Steam Laundry and Swan baths renowned for its youth swimming teams. Their pool was gently warmed by the rush of the water discharged into the river from the laundry after being used in the laundering process.

A seldom-seen view of Duke Street *c.*1904. The second palace of the Duke of Norfolk dating from 1602, which contained a playhouse, bowling alley and tennis court, straddled this area. After an altercation between the duke and the mayor regarding the duke's company of comedians, the nobleman flew into a fit of rage and ordered a portion of his palace be pulled down. Most of the palace was demolished in 1711 and after further demolition in 1806, a resolution was made to cut a road and build a bridge in this area, a project which became a reality in 1822.

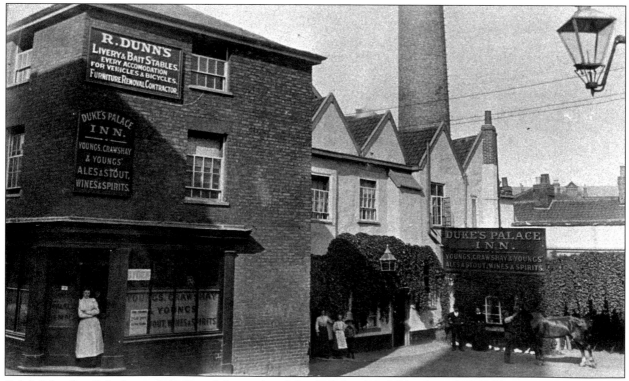

Duke's Palace Inn, Duke Street *c.*1890. Part of the remains of the old Duke of Norfolk's palace, which had been used as a workhouse, became an inn in the early 19th century. A popular place of entertainment in its early years, it hosted Polito's famous 'world beasts' exhibition, which included 'A He-lion' and 'A Hunting Tygar'. In later years its sale room acted as a cinema, but time was not kind to the old inn and it was finally demolished in 1968.

Duke Street from near the railings of St Mary's Church, 1958. Slick 'Teddy boy' haircuts and long dark coats are the order of the day. On the street on the left is Hipperson's bicycle shop and just beyond that is the old tobacconist and sweet shop. Just up the road on the right, the large building with the fine viewing gallery was the Crome Central School and Municipal Secondary School opened in 1888. Closing after World War Two, it became the Duke Street Centre for Sports and Leisure until 1995. Today it has returned to educational use and is part of the Norwich College of Art and Design.

The St Michael at Coslany end of Colegate Street, c.1950. Still an area of many fine 16th and 17th-century buildings under the care of civic authorities and preservation trusts. The gabled café beside Queen Anne Yard is now a private house and stands as a fine testament to the restorer's art. The Georgian building beside it was unceremoniously demolished in the 1960s but has been replaced by modern retail premises and apartments, almost in keeping.

Oak Street with the tower of St Michael at Coslany Church head and shoulders over the rooftops *c*.1930. At the turn of the century Oak Street was a community consisting of more than 40 yards with such delightful names as Flower Pot, Ragged School, Arabian Horse and Little Brew. There was also nine malthouses, two churches, a mission hall, the St Miles's Girls' and Infants' National School, a few pubs and, in 1913, even a cinema, the Empire. Through war damage and demolition of slums, poor old Oak Street was not preserved for future generations; very few of the structures along its length today pre-date 1950.

Barn Road at the junctions of Westwick Street (left) and Heigham Street (right). The gable end just visible to the left is of the building known as the Monkey House which was moved piece by piece from Whitlingham in 1900. This along with the Railway Stores and every building seen on this photograph was either blown up or burnt out in the 1942 blitz. The inner link road rushes traffic through this area today.

A seldom seen photograph of Grapes Hill *c.*1900. One of the rarest images in this collection this not only shows the tower of the Roman Catholic Church under construction but the quiet little road named after the Grapes pub which wound its way beside the city walls up this hill. Severely damaged in the blitz, what was left was pulled down in the 1960s to make way for a four-lane road system which has become one of the busiest parts of the inner link road.

The scene of devastation speaks for itself. This is the great crater at St Benedict's Gates on 30 April 1942. Over the preceding two nights some 297 high-explosive bombs and thousands of incendiaries had rained down on the city. A total of 231 people were killed and 689 wounded.

Dereham Road looking towards St Benedict's Gates *c.*1910. On the right, on the corner of Charles Street is the Primitive Methodist Chapel with its bold hoarding advertising 'Children's Days of Praise'. This chapel, along with a number of houses, were severely damaged in June 1942 when a stick of incendiary bombs were dropped on the area.

Looking up Dereham Road away from the city at the junction with Old Palace Road (right) and Heigham Road (left) *c.*1910. One of the classic long entrance roads to Norwich, it was marked at both the beginning and end by a pub, the Barn and the Gatehouse respectively. The Gatehouse remains to this day. On the right is the Dial, another pub that once stood along this road.

The Dereham Road/Barn Road/Grapes Hill and St Benedict's crossroads with policeman on point duty, 1954. In the austere years after World War Two few could afford a car and most city folks got to work on a bicycle or walked. In these days when most household have at least one car, it now takes numerous sets of traffic lights to do the job of the one officer in this hectic area. In the background is the Regal cinema (1938-58) offering the delights of *Quo Vadis* 'next week'. Redundant for a number of years it has recently been converted to the City Arms, a smart J.D. Wetherspoons pub.

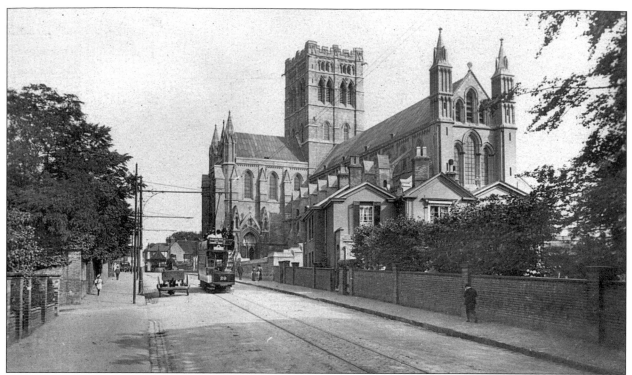

Earlham Road showing the newly-completed Roman Catholic Church, c.1913. This magnificent church was built between 1884 and 1912 with finance from the 15th Duke of Norfolk. The church was given cathedral status by the Vatican on 13 March 1976 and its first bishop was enthroned on 2 June the same year.

The Tuns pub is affectionately remembered by the people of Norwich. It stood on the corner of Unthank Road at the junction of Grapes Hill and St Giles Street and is pictured here c.1950. The Tuns once vied with the Adam and Eve for the title of the oldest licensed premises in Norwich, but analysis of samples from the beams in the oldest part of the pub revealed that it was a mere 400 years old. Since the inner link carved through the city, the Tuns appears to sit on the brow of a hill. Unhappily, the Tuns' name was changed to Temple Bar in recent years.

St Giles Gates viewed from Unthank Road *c*.1930. It is a difficult view to put into perspective today after widespread demolition and construction to facilitate the provision of a roundabout for the inner link road here in the 1960s. On the left is the wall and part of the Roman Catholic Church. Further down the road can be seen the distinctive upper-storey bow window of the Tuns. The rest of the houses along Unthank Road in the foreground have been heavily restored or demolished, while those beyond at St Giles Gates were mercilessly demolished.

St Giles Gates, viewed from Upper St Giles *c*.1955. Prior to the construction of the inner link road, this area had a good selection of city shops such as barbers, tobacconists and general stores. After being spoilt by the inner link road, it enjoyed a great revitalisation in the late 1970s and into the 1990s with specialist delicatessens, good quality restaurants, antiquarian bookshops and galleries. Due to a number of recent closures, most notably the long-established and respected Crowe's bookshop, city authorities should be mindful that this area should not be allowed to decline.

St Giles Street, 1962. On the right is the strong frontage of the old Norwich Union Fire Insurance Society Limited (Accident Branch). It was built over the old premises of 41-43 St Giles shortly after the turn of the last century in a style to complement their Surrey Street headquarters designed by G.J. and F.W. Skipper. St Giles Street has changed little and is well worth a visit for its excellent shops and restaurants.

W.J. Boddy & Son Ltd, agricultural ironmongers of 35 St Giles Street, pictured in 1968. A traditional Norwich family business, it was founded in 1902 by Mr W.J. Boddy in St George's and he was joined by his son about eight years later. Concentrating on agricultural ironmongery they were probably the first retailers of milking machines in the county, for which they received a Royal Warrant in 1955. The little shop in St George's was destroyed in an air-raid in August 1942 so a move was considered best and the premises on St Giles was considered very suitable. Time moved on and Boddy's became more of a thing of the past; such shops were growing fewer and fewer around the city centre and, despite always having an artistic and fascinating window display, they sadly closed in the 1990s.

The Grand Opera House, St Giles Street *c.*1903. Built by a syndicate led by leading investors and Messrs Bostock and Fitt, it opened in 1903. This magnificent theatre, built in the Renaissance style, was designed by London architect W.G.R. Sprague and could seat 2,000 people. Soon changing its name to the Hippodrome, it became one of Norfolk's premier music halls and vaudeville theatres. Many leading performers appeared here, including Laurel and Hardy, and Tommy Trinder. Poltician David Lloyd George spoke here, and the Hippodrome also presented some of the first bioscope films seen in Norfolk. The theatre closed for the last time in 1960 and was demolished in 1966 to make way for a multi-storey car park.

Posed 'front of house' (note the prices of 3s for dress circle, 2s 6d for stalls and 1s 6d for balcony) at the Grand Opera House on St Giles Street, here is a full line-up of the Norwich Amateur Operatic Society cast for Gilbert and Sullivan's *Princess Ida*, performed at 1908. The scene is flanked by commissionaires and theatre staff and completed by Mr Bostock and Mr Fitt seated centre of the front row in their evening dress.

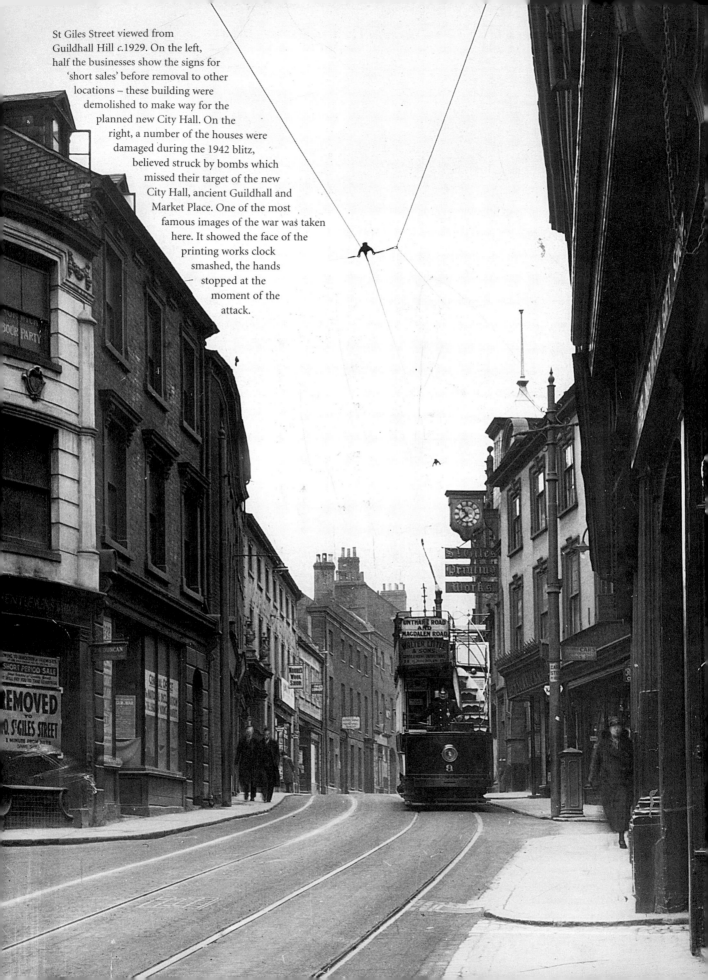

St Giles Street viewed from Guildhall Hill *c*.1929. On the left, half the businesses show the signs for 'short sales' before removal to other locations – these building were demolished to make way for the planned new City Hall. On the right, a number of the houses were damaged during the 1942 blitz, believed struck by bombs which missed their target of the new City Hall, ancient Guildhall and Market Place. One of the most famous images of the war was taken here. It showed the face of the printing works clock smashed, the hands stopped at the moment of the attack.

Chapel Field Drill Hall *c.*1914. Opened in 1866 by HRH the Prince of Wales, it was to serve the volunteer and territorial forces of the city. Through recruitment drives in two world wars, thousands of local lads joined the colours here to 'do their bit'. Despite its strong links with the city's past, the Drill Hall was demolished in 1963, another victim of the inner link road.

Chapel Field Gardens *c.*1905. This was originally an open ground used for archery practice and the training of the city artillery in the 16th century. In the 18th century a large area of Chapelfield was flooded to create a reservoir. Drained in the mid-19th century it was laid out by the corporation and opened to the public as pleasure gardens in 1880. The iron pagoda (left) was made as an exhibition piece by Barnard's iron foundry at the turn of the 20th century. By 1948 it had become unstable and was taken down.

Parasols and straw hats to the fore at a Sunday afternoon concert from the pavilion on Chapel Field Gardens, *c.*1895.

Caley's delivery vans in front of Chapel Field Works in 1921. A local business which manufactured mineral waters, crackers and chocolate, Caley's was sold out of family hands in 1918. After passing through the hands of African & Eastern Trading Corporation and John Mackintosh & Sons it was eventually sold to Nestlé who closed the factory in 1997. There is some consolation however, some of the senior managers bought the Caley trademark and are successfully producing Caley's chocolate in the city today.

Firemen struggle to put out the fire after Caley's factory on Chapelfield was firebombed on the night of 28-29 April 1942. It was not exactly a key target – the most offensive material made by the factory for the war effort was their famous 'Marching Chocolate' of a fine bitter-sweet consistency. The factory was built anew and the smell from the vats of warm chocolate soon filled the city air again.

The Theatre Royal, 1934. The first theatre on this site was built in 1758 as a concert hall by Sir Thomas Ivory. Successful and requiring enlargement, it was demolished and the new, improved and enlarged Theatre Royal was opened on 26 March 1826. These old buildings were destroyed by a terrible fire not long after this photograph was taken. It was rebuilt and opened again on 30 September 1935, but most of the buildings we see today date from the theatre refurbishments of 1971 and the 1990s.

The Theatre Royal, 2002. The closure of this theatre through lack of funding in 1990 shocked so many people that it was not long before a serious rescue package was put in motion and fronted by the one man who never lost faith in the great theatre's future – its general manager, Mr Dick Condon. With a twinkle in his eye and a ready wit, this charismatic Irishman did so much to bring people back to the theatre, but he died just before the Theatre Royal reopened in 1992. Let us hope that its continuing success and enthusiastic management prove to be a fitting memorial to Dick Condon.

The Assembly House, Theatre Plain, 1979. Once one of the largest townhouses in Norwich, the Assembly House was purchased to become 'a public place of entertainment for county and city'. It was remodelled by Sir Thomas Ivory, to the building we would recognise today, in 1754. Bought and used by the Norwich Freemasons until the 1870s, it housed the Norwich High School for Girls until 1933, when the building was left empty. It opened again in 1950 as a popular venue for public meetings, recitals and small musical performances, as well as fine meals served in its restaurant. Badly damaged by fire in 1995, it has recently been lovingly restored to its former glory.

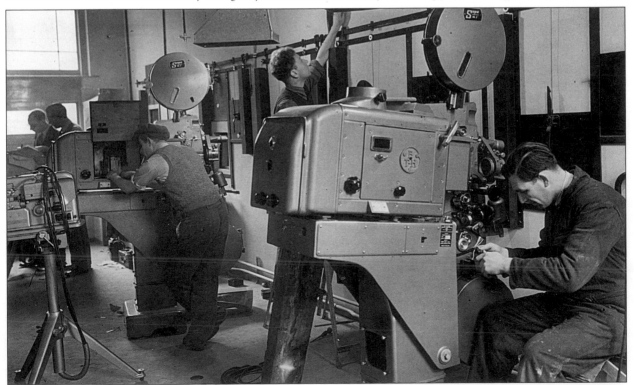

A bustling projection room getting ready for the first show at the Noverre Cinema 1950. Tucked away in a corner by the Assembly House was the entrance to this, one of the most 'personal' cinemas in the city. Only capable of seating 272 in its converted ballroom auditorium it was a great cinema for films not generally available on the commercial circuit. After declining numbers over four years the Noverre closed with a full house on 23 December 1992.

Probably the earliest photograph in this collection, this shows the Swan Inn on Theatre Street *c*.1855. Known as the White Swan in the 18th century, in the days before Ivory's Theatre Royal, this was 'the principal temple of Thespis' in the city. It was also the headquarters of the Norwich Company of Comedians from 1730. Once entertainments passed to the purpose-built theatre, the White Swan built its reputations on passing shows and inter-county cockfights. This whole historic area was pulled down in the 1960s to make way for the new library and car park. All that remains today is the large and handsome church of St Peter Mancroft, but that is seen today with its 'pepper pot' angle pinnacles and central flèche which were added during the church restorations of the early 1880s.

Bethel Street and the tower of St Peter Mancroft Church *c.*1931 The opposite side of this little part of the street was torn down along with St Peter's Street and the old Municipal Buildings to make way for the new City Hall in the 1930s. On the corner was Misses Mann's furriers, next door the King's Arms pub, and side by side James Ayton and Walter Pratt cycles agents on the corner of Lady Lane where Richard Hearne, TV's 'Mr Pastry' was born.

The Mancroft Restaurant on the corner of Bethel Street and St Peter's Street *c.*1930. This whole area of Georgian inns and old shops was demolished less than five years later to make way for the new City Hall and fire station.

Bethel Street fire station with tenders and appliances, pictured in 1941. At the time the most modern fire station in the county, it was built at a cost of £33,372 and was opened by Alderman F.C. Jex, Lord Mayor of Norwich, on 9 November 1934.

The dying moments of Norwich Central Library are caught on film as the fire blazes inside on 1 August 1994. Most of the lending library was totally destroyed but most tragic was the destruction of large portions of the second ADA Memorial Library and the local studies collection, particularly that covering the city of Norwich. The author is very proud to say he was the first independent historian to pledge his help to rebuild the local studies collection and has been involved with the reconstitution of that collection ever since.

The Forum, officially opened by HM Queen Elizabeth II in July 2002. This is Norwich's latest public building and, like its neighbour the City Hall, its architecture has been a point of controversy, but rather like City Hall I believe the appeal of this new building will endure. It is certainly far more appealing than the building it replaced. The Forum contains the new library; Origins, a centre telling the history of the city and county in modern and interesting ways; there are also plans for BBC Television and local radio to be based here in the near future.